POWER TO
change

THE KESWICK
YEAR BOOK **2016**

PETER LEWIS

ADRIAN HOLLOWAY

JONATHAN LAMB

RAY EVANS

CALISTO ODEDE

BILL BYGROVES

BECOMING LIKE GOD'S SON

SIMON MANCHESTER

STEVE BRADY

DAVID JACKMAN

DEREK TIDBALL

RICO TICE

JEREMY McQUOID

First published 2017

British Library Cataloguing-in-Publication Data
A catalogue record for this book is available from the British Library.

ISBN: 978-1-78359-573-0
eBook ISBN: 978-1-78359-574-7

Set in Dante 12.5/16pt
Typeset in Great Britain by CRB Associates, Potterhanworth, Lincolnshire
Printed and bound in Great Britain by Ashford Colour Press Ltd, Gosport, Hampshire

Contents

The Bible Readings

Other Addresses

Introduction

The Keswick movement began over 140 years ago, and has rippled around the world since its early beginnings in the small Lake District town in the north of England, which gave it its name. There has been no slick marketing or central organization, but it has grown as a spiritual movement shaped by clear biblical priorities. In the summer of 2016, not only did we welcome nearly 15,000 Christians from around the UK and Europe, but also delegates from 11 other countries where Keswick ministry is underway – across Asia, Africa, North America, Europe, Australasia and the Caribbean.

Why has the movement caught the imagination of God's people globally? Why has it changed hearts and minds, energized local churches, and inspired the cause of global mission? Perhaps the answer lies in its clear focus:

the longing to see God's plan fulfilled that Christians should become like His Son. Christlikeness is the will of God for the people of God.

This was the central theme of the 2016 Convention, and perhaps this explains why there was such a warm spiritual response to the teaching of God's Word across the three weeks. Meeting in churches or marquees, in the cinema or Costa Coffee, our shared concern was to hear God's Word and to learn what it means to live a life like Christ's. Today, Christians around the world long to experience this reality. We sense the many pressures on the Christian community; we know the pull of sin in our lives; and we see the advance of secularism and pluralism which make it such hard going for the rising generation of believers. So the theme of spiritual renewal and growth in Christlikeness could not be more relevant.

There's no question that the 2016 Convention was a bumper year with most venues at bursting point. This was wonderful. But as we reflect on the event, we are grateful to God for more than just numbers. We thank Him that children grew in their faith and their understanding; that young people gave their lives to Christ; that missionaries from around the world were refreshed and re-envisioned; that the international Keswick movement was strengthened; that families and local churches were encouraged; that many were called into God's mission; and that hundreds committed themselves to live their lives under God's Word and in the power of his Spirit. For all this we praise God.

The book you now hold in your hands represents a small sample of the Bible teaching we received, and it is our hope that it will in some sense convey the penetrating impact of the Word and the Spirit that was experienced in Keswick over those summer weeks. We would especially like to encourage you to pursue the subject still further, and there are several ways to do this.

First, all the Bible teaching is available from Essential Christian, in various formats, and so please do visit their site and order materials for personal use, for your family, or for your church, using the link: http://www.eden.co.uk/keswick-convention/. Many churches use the Keswick DVDs for home group discussion, and you might like to consider this too. The main teaching given morning and evening is also available free of charge if you wish to download mp3s from our Keswick Ministries website, at the following link: https://keswickministries.org/resources/keswick-talk-downloads. Clayton TV also hosts a great backlist of teaching from Keswick, and you can find that here: http://www.clayton.tv

Second, please consider buying two books published especially for the 2016 Convention. These are made available under our *Keswick Resources* imprint, in partnership with IVP. The first is *Becoming Christlike*, by Peter Lewis, which is a wonderfully practical introduction to the theme (http://www.ivpbooks.com/keswick-resources-books/). And the second is *Transformed: Becoming Like God's Son* by Derek Tidball, which is ideal for personal study and for home groups, with seven key passages containing carefully crafted questions, from which your church will benefit greatly (http://www.ivpbooks.com/keswick-study-guides/). These and other Keswick resources books are available from IVP.

Third, if you do not already do so, why not think about joining us at Keswick each summer? There is a great programme year by year, accessible to people of all ages and backgrounds, and the details can be found on our website: www.keswickministries.org

As you read these passages, may you encounter the living Lord, and commit yourself to becoming more like Him.

Jonathan Lamb
Minister-at-large, Keswick Ministries

Ephesians: Power to Change

How Are We Made New?

by Peter Lewis

Peter Lewis has recently retired after forty-five years as the senior pastor of the Cornerstone Church, Nottingham. During Peter's ministry, and with a growing ministry team, the church grew from an obscure, down-town church of fifty to a city-centre church of over 700 including 200 children, sent out many missionaries, and taught generations of students. Peter has written several books including *The Glory of Christ*, *The Message of the Living God*, *The Lord's Prayer*, *God's Hall of Fame*, and this year's Keswick Foundation title, *Becoming Christlike*. He is married to Valerie and they have two sons and two grandchildren.

How Are We Made New?
Ephesians 2:1–10

One of the most profound and agitated questions of our time is, 'Is there a purpose to my life, is there a plan?' And, 'Do I want a plan? Can I have any freedom if I believe that there is a plan, and can I have any real peace or satisfaction if I believe there isn't?'

A few years ago the Christian apologist Ravi Zacharias visited the Wexner Center for the Performing Arts which is on the campus of Ohio State University. When you enter the building you encounter 'stairways that go nowhere, pillars that hang from the ceiling without touching the floor, and angled surfaces configured to create a sense of vertigo. The architect, we are duly informed, designed this building to reflect life itself – senseless and incoherent – and what he referred to as "the capriciousness of the rules that organize the built world."'[1]

When the rationale was explained to Ravi Zacharias he had just one question for the guide: 'Did he do the same with the foundation?'[1]

The point of course was that the architect would not have dreamt of putting his philosophy into real practice because actually the rules of 'the built world' are not capricious. There is such a thing as purpose, order, design that works, and to ignore it would soon be fatal. The message of the Bible is that life is not an accident and God is not capricious. God does have a plan, a plan that centres on Jesus Christ and includes each of us.

In his great letter to the Ephesian Christians Paul begins by introducing us to this plan of God. It was a plan laid out in eternity to share his eternal life with other beings; a human race made in his image, for his glory and to share his joy. It would be a plan that would cost God dear and plunge him into the world's cruelty, injustice and pain. Why? 'For God so loved the world that he gave his one and only Son, that whoever believes in him shall not perish but have eternal life' (John 3:16). The achievement of that Son would be the redemption of millions and the extent of it would be the bringing together of heaven and earth.

For us tonight the astounding truth is that this great plan of salvation has come down to our door and involves us. We were part of the world's rebellion but Jesus Christ has become our peace.

Many people find Christianity threatening because of its insistence on facing sin as an issue in all our lives. Some have dismissed Christianity as dangerous and unhealthy because it 'lays guilt' on people. I want to show that this Christian message, when it's truly Christian and not distorted, is realistic, supremely liberating and thoroughly healthy.

It *is* true that the Christian message presents us with very uncomfortable truths; but inasmuch as they *are* truths they are important, if life is to make sense and to have meaning. Thank God that the good news, the gospel, brings us face to face with our Saviour as well as our sin, and speaks a message of reliable hope in a world where false hopes fail daily.

But to understand the importance of this good news, we have to face up to the bad news. People don't go in for surgery for every ache or pain, but when the X-ray shows a growing tumour they can't get surgery quickly enough. 'The main human trouble is desperately difficult to fix, even for God, and sin is the longest-running of human emergencies.'[2] The apostle Paul is going to use the most extreme language to tell us the seriousness of our condition and the wonder of God's achievement in our world. In Ephesians 2:1–3 he writes:

> As for you, you were dead in your transgressions and sins, in which you used to live when you followed the ways of this world and of the ruler of the kingdom of the air, the spirit who is now at work in those who are disobedient. All of us also lived among them at one time, gratifying the cravings of our flesh and following its desires and thoughts. Like the rest, we were by nature deserving of wrath.

It's all summed up in those first words: 'As for you, you were dead in your transgressions and sins.' 'Transgressions' speak of a deliberate crossing of a boundary, a defiance of law, in this case a defiance of God's law and so a defiance of God who gives it. The word 'transgressions' carries the idea of rebellion against God. This is at the heart of every human being. By nature we too were rebels unwilling to let God be Lord of our lives, determined to go our own way, defying his laws, claiming to be a law unto ourselves.

Sin is not properly understood until it is seen in terms of our relationship with God our Creator and his lordship in our lives. A life in sin is not necessarily an openly scandalous one: it might be a very respectable, useful, even admired one. But if it is godless, if God is not at the centre in his lordship, it is profoundly sinful. Sin is rebellion against God, where self is central and supreme. Always remember that sin is not simply a broken code but a broken relationship, not only a relationship lost but a relationship renounced. God de-centralized and self-enthroned; the worship of God denied and the worship of 'self' confirmed daily, this is the root of all human sin. Twentieth-century historian, Arnold Toynbee, surveyed twenty-six civilizations across the sweep of history, and after twelve volumes of close study he too concluded that self-worship is *the* religion of mankind, though it takes different forms.[3]

'Dead in your sins', verse 1, means dead toward God, separated from him and without the eternal life he gives. It means guilty and condemned, with a guilt that cannot be denied and a condemnation which cannot be removed by any human means: not by tears, not by good works, not by religious practices, not by therapy or mysticism. You are utterly helpless to save yourself.

But something has happened in our world in complete contrast to its long story of human sin, failure and death. God did a new thing, he sent a new man. Verses 4–7 of our passage read:

> But because of his great love for us, God, who is rich in mercy, made us alive with Christ even when we were dead in transgressions – it is by grace you have been saved. And God raised us up with Christ and seated us with him in the heavenly realms in Christ Jesus, in order that in the coming ages he might show the incomparable riches of his grace, expressed in his kindness to us in Christ Jesus.

The apostle Paul here, and elsewhere, teaches us that we have been taken up into a great event, the greatest event in the history of the world and even in the history of God himself. That event is the Christ-event: the life, death and resurrection of the Son of God. Into our world there came someone *like* us yet *unlike* us, someone who claimed to be the Son of God and the light of the world, someone who said he would give his life a ransom for many. 'In him', said Paul earlier, 'we have redemption, the forgiveness of sins' (Ephesians 1:7).

We must always remember the foundational teaching of the first chapter of Ephesians: that the Son of God came into our world and took to himself a human nature in order to act as the head and representative of his people, including ourselves. He represented us in his sinless life and he represented us in his atoning death; he represented us in his glorious resurrection and he represents us at the right hand of his Father in heaven.

At every point where we failed he succeeded – and he did so on our behalf. He lived the life we could not live and he died the death we could not die. He took our place under the *judgment* of God and he guarantees our place in the *glory* of God.

And the one who died for us has been raised for us. We can rightly say that Jesus rose from the dead. That is true. But eleven times in the Book of Acts it is proclaimed: '*God* raised him from the dead'. It was not an independent act. It was an act of God, and that is how we should tell it, placing the resurrection of Jesus in the context of God's truth and power.

And the resurrection on the first Easter Sunday morning was the victory-shout of God amplifying to the whole world what he said at Jesus' baptism: 'You are my Son, whom I love; with you I am well pleased' (Luke 3:22). The words of an ancient prophecy were never more wonderfully fulfilled: 'You are my Son . . . ask of me and I will make the nations your inheritance' (Psalm 2:8). And he *did* ask and the Father *has* given . . . And here *we* are today: you and I! We who were far off have been brought near by the blood of Christ. We who were dead made alive to God, made his sons and daughters by the adoption of grace, made alive with Jesus in his resurrection power which will never leave us but take us to heaven.

This is the wonderful story in each of our lives: at our conversions, indeed at the moment of new birth, the Spirit of God, the Holy Spirit, comes into our heart, reaches into the core of our being, and unites us to the living Christ. Sent by the risen, glorified Christ the Holy Spirit comes to live in each child of God. The Holy Spirit unites the sinner on earth with the Saviour in heaven. He himself is the link: permanent, unbreakable, and utterly adequate.

In that act of union and incorporation we become Christ's people, his body, part of his very identity as our head and representative. Christ takes each of us up into his own life, so that his past becomes our past and his future our future. Think of that: a new past. No one else can give you that. Nothing can alter your past. Someone may change your present or your future but everyone is helpless to change your past. But here is one who can give you a new past: the risen Christ, who lifts you into his past, and gives you a new future, who gives you a new identity and place in him. In him we are no longer chained to a great defeat (either Adam's or our own), no longer trapped in a doomed world, no longer bound to a great condemnation. Instead we share his past: his perfect obedience and his once-for-all atonement for sin, his resurrection and his heavenly life and glory with the Father.

And what an effect that has had on us and our former way of life. In Christ we have 'died to the old life', the old alliance of the world against God, the old allegiance to sin and self, the old standards and values. Now we have a new life, a new outlook, a new Lord and a new allegiance. Now the old has gone, the new has come.

I remember hearing, many years ago, a true story which dramatically illustrates this. Apparently there had been a revival in an obscure village in the mountains of a South American country. All the people of the village were Roman Catholics and the priest too had been part of the experience of God which had transformed the church and the lives of its worshippers.

The villagers wanted to mark the change that had taken place in their lives. The Church did not allow them to be re-baptized as adults but the priest had a brainwave. He got the village carpenter to construct a large coffin and put it at the front of the church. Then, in a special service, all those who had received the blessing came to the front one by one. Each of them were guided into the coffin. The lid was put down and then the priest knocked on the closed lid three times and said, 'In the name of the Father and of the Son and of the Holy Spirit.' The lid was opened and the person helped out to the cheers of the onlookers.

Someone later said if the coffin had been open and full of water it would have been perfect because that is the meaning of Christian baptism. Christian baptism signifies the believer's share in the death of Christ, the resurrection of Christ and the eternal life that followed from it: his life for us; our share in the future of God.

Here we struggle with many things: the pressures of life, our sins and our failures. But we do not struggle alone and unhelped. We struggle having this new life working within us; the life of the risen Christ brought to us and sustained in us by the Holy Spirit. We were dead in trespasses and sins but here is a death that brings life.

'It is by grace you have been saved', verse 5. Grace is one of the most important words in the Christian vocabulary. It's mentioned over one hundred times in the writings of Paul. It is at the very heart of the gospel. It is one of the mighty God-words of the Bible. Dr Packer calls it 'the keyword of Christianity'. What does it mean? Grace is the unmerited favour of God, his undeserved help, his free gift of salvation. The stress is always on the freeness of what is given. Grace speaks of God's initiative, patience, and love for the unworthy. Grace doesn't leave you desperately trying to earn the love of God, unsure and exhausted. Rather, it puts wings on your feet and a song in your heart knowing that nothing in life or death can separate you from this divine commitment.

It was grace that lifted the thief on the cross to heaven on the day Christ died for him and it is grace that still works in the hearts of the modern equivalents. Last year I read an extraordinary news item in *The Times*. Eight drug smugglers had spent years in an Indonesian jail awaiting execution; two were Australian, three were Nigerian and one each Brazilian, Indonesian and Ghanaian. In that time they had convincingly opened their hearts to the gospel and received instruction in Christian faith and life. The article began:

> The eight condemned drug smugglers chose to face their executioners, refusing the offer of hoods. Electing to stand rather than kneel or sit, they were shackled to wooden crosses, their arms outstretched. And in the final moments, before a firing squad of more than 100 Indonesian marksmen opened fire, the men sang 'Amazing Grace'. They also sang 'Bless the Lord O my Soul' before the song was cut off by the crack of gunfire.
> (*The Times* 30/04/2015)

One of the pastors present said, 'It was breath-taking.' Grace, the triumph of grace!

But there is more. Grace is not merely an *attitude in* God, it is an *action by* God. It is not only his activity at the start of our Christian lives lifting us out of condemnation, it is also his on-going activity in our lives. Grace is an energy-charged word throughout the Christian life. It is *God in action* in our lives: in our days and nights, in our advances and our set-backs, in our victories and in our defeats, in our youth and in our age.

And as such it means God isn't finished with you yet. Grace is an on-going work and not simply an initial push. Grace is God, who began a good work in us, continuing it all the way to completion. Grace is God at work persistently in our lives and hearts enabling us, empowering us, encouraging us. In verse 10 Paul writes, 'We are God's handiwork, created in Christ Jesus to do good works, which God prepared in advance for us to do.' The Jerusalem Bible famously translates that phrase, 'We are God's work of art'. A work in progress certainly, very unfinished and incomplete. But God himself is at work in us, conforming us more perfectly into the image of his Son. Developing that image, deepening that image, growing us, maturing us, perfecting us. He is like a sculptor chiselling away, getting rid of the surplus and the useless. God's been chipping away at me for years and I'm glad he hasn't stopped – aren't you?

At our conversions we are baby believers, callow saints, full of inconsistencies, and with areas of real weakness. So he continues the work he has begun. Sanctification is our growth in holiness, our resemblance to God, our family image. God, who sets us apart for himself at the start, claims more and more of our lives and sets that apart too, saying, 'I want this area of your life and that and that.' Only when we are sanctified are we safe. Every unsanctified area of your life is a danger area, a gap in your defences, a wound open to disease and ruin. It may be a relationship which is unwise, forbidden or abused. It may be an element in your character or behaviour which is potentially harmful to you or others. It may be a stage in your career, a talent, an opportunity. And God says, 'I want that and I want it now.'

God, you see, is in the business of changing people. He's not a static observer, an invigilator in life's exam or a marker at the end. He is an active participator, saying, 'I myself will be with you. I myself will sanctify you through and through.' What a transition, what a change! From dead in trespasses and sins to alive in Christ; from following the course of this world to reigning with Christ in the heavenly realms; from an object of wrath to a dearly loved child; from a life lost, to a work of art deepened, developed and perfected through eternal ages.

Our passage ends: 'We are God's handiwork, created in Christ Jesus to do good works, which God prepared in advance for us to do.' We are back to the plan of God again, a plan laid down in eternity, a plan which included you from the start. And here Paul tells us that God has not only planned our existence but our lives in Christ and the good works he calls us to. Think of that as you prepare to go home and when you get home. There are situations, opportunities, challenges which God has planned and is preparing you for. And he will be with you there and he will give you what you need to serve and glorify him. He will give you wisdom, an honest heart, strength for the day and blessing at its close. The plan for your life is written – play your part well.

Notes

1. Graham Johnson, *Preaching to a Postmodern World* (IVP, 2002), p. 82.
2. Cornelius Plantinga Jr, *Not the Way It's Supposed to Be – A Breviary of Sin* (Eerdmans, 2009), p. 5.
3. Raymond C. Ortlund, *Isaiah: God Saves Sinners* (Crossway, 2005), p. 129.

What Does Holiness Look Like?

by Adrian Holloway

Formerly a reporter for *The Times* newspaper in London, Adrian Holloway became a BBC radio and TV presenter. He has written two best-selling evangelistic novels, *The Shock of Your Life*, and the sequel, *Aftershock*. He presents the gospel to people who don't normally go to church all over Britain and enjoys speaking at UCCF carol services and university CU events weeks. He is based with his wife Julia and their four daughters at Everyday Church, a multi-site church in south-west London.

What Does Holiness Look Like?
Ephesians 4:17–32

I thought I'd begin by telling you how I first got together with Julia, who is now my wife.

There were about twenty of us friends who went ice skating. I really liked Julia, but I was absolutely convinced that she wouldn't like me, for one very good reason . . . I thought she was too good-looking for me. (This fact was confirmed by all my friends!) But I was one of the four nominated drivers for the trip and, not only did she get into my car, she actually sat next to me! But I didn't think that meant anything. I thought, 'She just wants to go ice skating.' The first time I fell over on the ice I could see Julia out of the corner of my eye laughing at me. But the next time I fell over, she came over to help me up. 'Ooh, what does that mean?' I wondered. But at the time, I thought, 'She just feels sorry for me.'

But then at the end of the day, all twenty of us went back to someone's house to watch a video. Julia was the last person to enter the room and not only did she sit on my side of the room, she actually chose to sit on the carpet right next to the chair that I was sitting in. In fact, looking back, I probably should have offered her my chair!

And that was the first moment when I thought, 'Maybe the seemingly impossible dream that Julia Brown would like me is coming true!' It was an electric feeling. You know, I've only had that same electric feeling on one other occasion in my life, and that was on the day when I began a relationship with God.

Coming to know God through trusting Jesus Christ has been so good that it's natural that as a result, verse 31 says I should 'Get rid of all bitterness.' When I got the invitation from the Keswick committee and read the passage, I asked myself, had I got rid of *all* bitterness? The answer was 'No'. I thought maybe I could email the Keswick committee back and ask for a *different* passage? And then I thought of an ingenious way to solve the problem: 'What if, Adrian, you obeyed the text! What, if Adrian, you got rid of *all* bitterness?'

And there was more in verse 32: 'Be kind and compassionate to one another, forgiving each other, just as in Christ God forgave you.' And I immediately thought of one person who I had not totally forgiven. You see, I'm very keen on total forgiveness when it comes to God forgiving me. I love the fact that at the cross all my sins have been forgiven. I am so glad that God has totally forgiven me for everything I have ever done wrong. But had I totally forgiven the person who, I think, wronged me? Had I forgiven that person, just as in Christ God forgave me? No, no I hadn't.

And I wanted to try and understand why I hadn't got rid of 'all bitterness'. How come I had not totally forgiven that other person after all the forgiveness I've received from God? I'd been a Christian for so long, how could there still be bitterness and unforgiveness that I had to deal with before I could stand on this platform to preach this text?

And I found the answer to my question right in the middle of this passage. Our passage tonight is going to take us in three directions. Paul wants us to . . .

1. Look out at how non-believers behave (verses 17–19)
2. Look back at what Jesus has already done for us (verses 20–24)
3. Look at our own thinking so that our new life produces a new lifestyle (verses 25–32)

So firstly, we're told to look out at how non-believers behave. These Ephesian Christians were surrounded by full-blown idolatry. They'd grown up in it. And Paul describes the true nature of that old way of life in a series of devastating phrases that are reminiscent of Romans chapter 1. Paul shows us a landscape that is bleak and severe.

But notice that Paul doesn't start with the sensuality or the sexual indulgence that would have grabbed most people's attention. No, Paul regards that as no more than the logical outcome of a process that begins in the brain. It starts, verse 17, in the mind, with futile thinking, which leads, verse 18, to a darkened understanding. And we're going to see, in this passage, that God is tremendously interested in our thinking. The cause of Christ is so important that what's going on in my head and in your head really matters.

But next, in verse 20, we suddenly come out of the valley. Paul takes us right up to the top of a mountain so we can, secondly, look back at what Jesus has already done for us. Paul says to these Ephesians: 'you learned Christ' (verse 20), 'you heard' Christ (verse 21), and 'you were taught in him' (verse 21b). The NIV translation says 'you heard about Christ' but in the original Greek, the word 'about' is not there. These Ephesians didn't just hear 'about' Christ, they actually heard Christ.

And you say, 'That's ridiculous, Jesus never visited Ephesus, so how can Paul possibly say that these Ephesians heard Christ?' Oh, but they did. When they filed into the lecture hall of Tyrannus, they heard Christ. Paul was speaking yes, but they heard Christ. To paraphrase John Stott's commentary on these verses: Christ was the lesson, Christ was the teacher, and Christ was the school.[1]

They heard Christ. And so did you. It was your mother speaking, but you heard Christ. It was one Sunday night when you were sixteen years old, and an evangelist spoke, but you heard Christ. Or maybe it was here in this very tent, many years ago. Someone opened the Bible, and began to preach, but you heard Christ. It was real. Jesus is alive and you heard him speaking to you. And you were converted. You were born again. That was the end of the old you, and it was the start of the new you.

Which brings us to the heart of this passage in verses 22–24.

And when I was preparing for this evening, something very unusual happened. I found that all the commentators I most trust criticized the English translation of these verses. They all said that if your translation leaves you thinking that this putting off the old self in verse 22 and putting on the new self in verse 24 is something you've got to do in the future in order to earn God's acceptance, then it's a bad translation. If you've read those verses and you're feeling dejected because it looks like you're being told to pull your socks up, and change your behaviour in order to make yourself a Christian, it's a bad translation.

All the books, all the greats, were desperate to tell me that the putting off of the old self in verse 22 and the putting on of the new self in verse 24 are in the aorist tense, which is a tense we don't have in English. And, crucially, it is a past tense. It's something that has already happened. This is good news.

It's clear when we look at what Paul says in the parallel passage in Colossians 3:9–10:

> Do not lie to one another, seeing that you have put off the old self with its practices and have put on the new self, which is being renewed in knowledge after the image of its creator. (ESV)

The Colossian Christians are already Christians. They've put off the old self, and they've put on the new self. And the Ephesians are just the same.

But whereas the putting off of the old self in verse 22, and the putting on of the new self in verse 24 are past tense, by contrast, the infinitive in verse 23, 'to be made new in the attitude of your minds', is present tense. So in the past, at the cross, Christ made me acceptable to God. But now, present tense, I am being made new in the attitude of my mind. As Romans 12:2 reminds us, 'Do not conform to the pattern of this world, but be transformed by the renewing of your mind.' In other words, when you think about who Christ is, when you think about who you are in Christ, you fill your mind with your new identity in all its glory.

Pause here and consider the undeniable truth that you can choose your thoughts. I can choose to churn over in my mind negative thoughts or I can choose to take those thoughts captive to be obedient to Christ. I can then choose to think about something else – something good, something encouraging about who I am in Christ. So let's allow our new identity in Christ to work itself out in our behaviour. Let's thirdly: look at our own thinking so that our new life produces a new lifestyle.

Take for example, verse 26, where it's vital that I deal quickly with unrighteous anger. If I don't, if I dwell on what that person said to my wife, or my kids, then that anger can gain a foothold in my life. The commentators say that bitterness heads the list in verse 31 because it so often leads to the other sins that Paul names. Hebrews 12:15 says, 'See to it that no root of bitterness grows up.' Bitterness is under the surface, the root is not visible, no one else can see it. But can I ask you tonight, are you bitter about something that happened to you? If so, we need to remind ourselves about who God says we are in Christ. If we allow angry or negative thoughts to churn around in our heads, they lead to bitterness and bitterness leads to the other sins Paul mentions.

Can I ask you tonight, have you forgiven that other person, 'just as in Christ God forgave you'? I have to confess to you that I have committed the sin of unforgiveness. I have promised to *not* go around telling everyone about the wrong I believed was done to me. But suffice to say that I had never been hurt so intensely. And rather than feeling guilty about my unforgiving attitude, I thought my unforgiveness was OK because what they did was so bad.

But here in Ephesians 4, I'm told to forgive totally. To forgive just as in Christ, God forgave me. It was the toughest thing I had ever been asked to do. And for some of you, forgiving the person who hurt you will be the toughest thing you've ever been asked to do. You may have good reasons for feeling the way you do. You may have gone through things that no one deserves to experience in life. Maybe a good friend betrayed you and you have every reason to be angry and bitter.

We need to come to terms with the fact that we have been hurt. But nobody, not even God ever promised that *this* life would be fair. Tonight, the good news is that in verse 32, we see one huge positive incentive, one huge positive reason to forgive: 'Because in Christ, God forgave you.'

You see, Jesus did not just tell us to forgive. He gave us forgiveness. At the cross, you were totally forgiven. What does that mean? It means that you won't be punished for any of your sins. Nobody will know about your sins. God won't tell. When Peter is preaching in Acts 3:19 he talks about our sins being, 'wiped out'. Your sins have gone! Where? Where have these sins gone? What happened to them? They were taken by Jesus. The Bible says that the Lord has laid on him the sin, or the iniquity, of us all. 1 John 1:7 says that Jesus' blood cleanses us from all sin. You have received total forgiveness. That's why it's so liberating. That's why it's so freeing. Every single thing you've ever done wrong has been forgiven. And you did not deserve it.

You see our whole problem is that we think that the person who hurt us does not deserve to be forgiven. And for all I know, you're right, the person who hurt you does not deserve to be forgiven. But neither do I, and yet at the cross, God forgave me totally. And if you do forgive, you'll feel better. Holding a grudge doesn't make you happy. Replaying what they did to you doesn't make you feel better. It makes you feel worse. And slowly you become a bitter person. Have you ever tasted something bitter? It's like we're carrying around this poison, this toxic waste of unforgiveness.

And when we don't forgive, we're not hurting the other person, we're only hurting ourselves. For your emotional and spiritual health, you can't afford to drink this poison any longer. You can't do anything about the past, but you can do something about your future. Don't let this poison contaminate your life. Say tonight: 'I refuse to drink the poison of unforgiveness.'

There was a beautiful village in Africa in a mountainous region. A small group lived together. They were a close community with a wonderful provision of clear drinking water from a mountain stream. One day, people noticed that the water had started to taste bitter. Then about two or three days later, people started to fall ill. It quickly became obvious that the water supply from the mountain stream had become contaminated. And so the elders got together to walk up the mountain to locate the source of the stream. They found the source in a cave and inside they discovered some pigs had got trapped and died. Their bodies had started to decompose and all the water flowing over the dead pigs was contaminating the water supply that the villagers were drinking. So the elders climbed into the cave, took the dead pigs out and burnt them. And do you know, the water returned to its crystal clear form. The people who were sick were healed and the villagers could drink from the stream once again.

That can happen to you tonight. If you'll begin to forgive the people who have offended you, and release all the hurt and pain, the bitterness will leave you and you'll begin to see that crystal-clear water flowing again. You can begin to experience the joy, peace and freedom that God intended you to have. You'll feel clean like a pure stream, no longer polluted by feelings of unforgiveness.

You might be saying: 'Adrian, you have absolutely no idea what they did to me. I can't do it. It's too hard. I just can't forgive. They hurt me too badly.' You are absolutely right, I don't know what they did to you. But here's the one thing that I do know about you: if you hold on to this cup, sometime in the future – maybe a week from now, a month from now, a year from now, or ten years from now – it is going to start feeling really heavy. And that is why tonight, verse 32 says, it's time to let it go! How can you enjoy all the benefits of living a victorious, overcoming, abundant Christian life, if you're carrying this unforgiveness? Let it go!

Live a life of forgiveness. Don't go around trying to pay people back, trying to get revenge. God sees every wrong that's been done to you. God sees every person who's ever hurt you. And he's keeping the record. God says: 'It is mine to avenge; I will repay' (Deuteronomy 32:35, see also Romans 12:19, Hebrews 10:30). So don't barge in on God's territory. If the person who hurt you should be punished in this life, God will do it. God will take care of what needs to be taken care of, don't step in and try and do it for him.

'OK', you say, 'let's imagine I don't drink the poison. What happens to the poison?' Well, on the night before he died, in the Garden of Gethsemane, Jesus was praying so hard that drops of blood fell from his forehead into the ground. And he was praying about this cup. Imagine arriving in the garden holding this cup which contains all the sins I've committed. I'm not perfect enough for a perfect heaven. The Bible says nothing impure can enter heaven (Revelation 21:27). So I cannot go to heaven when I die. Inside my cup are all my sins. All the times that I have hurt other people. I have to drink my own cup for that. And so there I am holding my cup. The Bible says: 'All have sinned and fall short of the glory of God . . . the wages of sin is death' (Romans 3:23; 6:23). If I drink this thing, I'll die.

Jesus meanwhile, over here, on the ground, Jesus has never sinned. He's never done anything wrong. Jesus didn't have a cup. So why is Jesus sweating drops of blood? Why is he agonizing about my cup and your cup? Because God the Father has asked Jesus to drink your cup and my cup. You see if God is going to be the just judge of the universe, he must punish sin. A just judge can't just pretend that sin doesn't exist or it doesn't matter. No, a just judge has to punish sin. The cup must be drunk. Your sin, my sin, can't just be ignored. And because God so loved you, the Father's plan is that Jesus drinks your cup instead of you.

And Jesus is in agony of soul, because he's being asked not just to drink your cup, but to drink down the sins of everyone who would ever believe. God's plan is that Jesus is to drink a massive cup of sin. And so Jesus prays: 'Father, if it's possible, let his cup be taken from me. Father, if there is any other way that Brian and Deborah, Robert and Sally can be saved, if there's any way they can have their sins forgiven and go to heaven without me having to go to the cross, then please let me avoid the cross, let me not have to drink the judgment for their sins, let this cup be taken away from me.'

But when he finished the prayer, the heavens were silent. There was no other way. And so Jesus magnificently says *yes* to the Father's plan. Jesus says: 'Father, there is no other way. I will go to the cross. I will drink the cup.' Jesus says: 'Not my will, but yours be done' (Luke 22:42). Jesus Christ was and is the only perfect person who has ever lived. He is the only person who is perfect enough for a perfect heaven. Jesus didn't have his own cup. He didn't have his own sins. And that's why it's so amazing that on the cross Jesus drank your cup. He drank my cup. And on the cross, an exchange, a swap, took place. Christ gave you his righteousness, his perfection, and then he drank the poison. And when he'd finished drinking the poison, taking all the punishment for all your sins, he said: 'It is finished!' He gave up his spirit and died.

Jesus drank the poison, so you don't have to. And tonight, if you haven't yet put your trust in Christ, you can. Jesus takes your sins, and he gives you his righteousness.

Note

1. John Stott, *The Message of Ephesians* (BST) (IVP, 1991), p. 179.

How Do I Overcome the Pull of Sin?

by Jonathan Lamb

Jonathan is the minister-at-large for Keswick Ministries, supporting the work in the UK and often speaking at other Keswicks around the world. He is the author, with Ian Randall, of *Knowing God Better: the Vision of the Keswick Movement*, and has also published a Keswick Foundation title *Preaching Matters: Encountering the Living God* (IVP). He also serves as a Vice President of IFES.

How Do I Overcome the Pull of Sin? Ephesians 5:1–14

Not long ago I read of a pilot who was practising high-speed manoeuvres in a jet fighter. He turned the controls for what he thought was a steep ascent, and he flew straight into the ground. He was unaware of the fact that he had been flying upside down.

That's something of a parable for our times, isn't it? Living at high speed, but with no clue whether we are upside down or the right-side up. That's the problem of living life without external reference points. Maybe you saw the discussion about a recent Government leaflet on sex education. The advice urged parents to avoid telling their children the difference between right and wrong. It should be values-free or values-lite. In an accompanying article in *The Times*, one clinical psychologist wrote: 'We do not know what is right and wrong; right and wrong is relative.' And gradually we move away from God's standards; we live life on our own terms. Most people now suspect that our society is simply making it up as it goes along. And, like the pilot flying at high speed, it has disastrous consequences.

Whatever happened to right and wrong? Whatever happened to sin, we might ask? It seems that in our culture it is ignored, trivialized or evaded. Sin is a word now used only on dessert menus in our restaurants – 'Death by Chocolate' is sin. Sometimes sin is celebrated, often in TV chat shows which provide a platform for people to confess their lurid sins with a certain pride, even to be applauded by an excited studio audience. And sin is excused – 'It's my background . . . my upbringing . . . my genes.' And this has impacted Christians too. We talk less about sin; we preach about it more infrequently. Where sin is concerned, we Christians mumble.

In the letter we're looking at, Paul has already exposed the root issues. In chapter 2 he wrote, 'As for you, you were dead in your transgressions and sins . . . you were by nature deserving of wrath' (verses 1, 3). Paul gives a radical diagnosis: our problem is a fundamental attitude of rebellion against God, an alienation from him which inevitably leads to his judgment. Here in chapter 5 there is a graphic description of the pull of sin. The verses describe a context which we easily recognize, a society which is drifting away from God. Paul describes behaviour which is completely alien to a Christian lifestyle, verse 3:

> But among you there must not be even a hint of sexual immorality, or of any kind of impurity, or of greed, because these are improper for God's holy people. Nor should there be obscenity, foolish talk or coarse joking, which are out of place, but rather thanksgiving.

Paul is concerned about Christian converts from a Gentile background who could easily slip back to their old way of life. In verse 3, 'sexual immorality and impurity' are terms which cover every kind of sexual sin. And 'greed' could relate to sexual sin too, but could also apply more widely. Greed is the insatiable desire to acquire more and more, whatever the object of that greed might be.

First-century Ephesus was awash with immorality, and we all know that this is completely dominant in our own culture too. It's seen in sexual immorality of all kinds. You can monitor the rapidly changing patterns of morality just by watching TV soaps, which can have a powerful influence on us. And for us believers, like those first-century converts, the pressure to lower our standards, to go with the flow of the culture, is constant. Verse 4 continues by insisting the problem is not only immorality in behaviour but also speech: 'nor should there be obscenity, foolish talk or coarse joking.' And in verse 12, Paul says these pagan ways of behaving should not be even mentioned or named. It's possible this means not simply that we shouldn't talk about them but that, when people look at us as Christians, they should have no excuse to name any such sin of immorality or greed amongst us. So in a few sentences Paul captures the insidious influence of sin: the immorality, impurity, and greed which pervade every corner of our society.

And the question we are looking at is hugely relevant for every one of us – *How can I overcome the pull of sin?* All of us are acutely aware of the struggle. We know that sin has a fatal attraction. It has truly deadly consequences. Well, embedded within this section of Ephesians, God has provided several wonderful incentives, some powerful motivations that will help us turn from sin and live for him. And it's important to notice that each has to do with what God has done.

1. I am loved by God the Father

Chapter 5 begins, 'Follow God's example, therefore, as dearly loved children.' The previous chapter ends by urging us to forgive, just as in Christ God forgave us. And that leads directly to the call in 5:1 to 'follow God's example' – to love as God has loved us. As we think about the pull of sin, verse 1 highlights why sinful behaviour is totally inconsistent for true believers. A fundamental reason for refusing to live immorally is that I am now God's dearly loved child. I've been adopted into God's family. His love has been poured out into my heart by the Holy Spirit. So I should imitate my Father, I should reproduce the family likeness.

Verses 3 and 4 describe self-gratification, the self-centred lust for more. The big characteristic of first-century pagan religion, and the twenty-first-century sex industry, is the emphasis on getting, not giving. Its definition of love is self-centred, its motivation is self-fulfilment not self-sacrifice. But if we know God as Father, then we will want to walk in the way of love. And because we share the Father's nature, we can exhibit the Father's character. That's our new identity. It's in our DNA.

In the heat of temptation, feeling the pull of sin, this is what we should say: 'I am loved by the Father.' If I'm tempted to look to sex or to greedy self-indulgence for satisfaction, I say, 'I am loved by the Father.' If I'm injured by someone and want to fight back, I say, 'I am loved by the Father.' If we focus on how we have been loved – eternally, irrevocably, freely – then we find we will have a growing desire to live for him. That's because love like this changes us. It draws us towards God, and it makes living for him something we are deeply committed to.

2. I belong to God's people

> But among you there must not be even a hint of sexual immorality, or of any kind of impurity, or of greed, because these are improper for God's holy people. (verse 3)

The exhortation to avoid immorality and impurity is based on the fact that we belong to God's holy people. We've been chosen; we are set apart. So the kind of behaviour described in verse 3 violates God's standards – it is improper for God's holy family. If we long to overcome the pull of sin, the question is: to whom or what do we ultimately belong? It's an issue of where our heart is.

Tim Chester's book on sexual temptation has a significant title and a positive emphasis – it's called *Captured by a Better Vision*. If you are loved by the Father, and if you belong to his holy people, your motivation has changed, you are captured by a better vision. I chatted with Matthew and Karen Sleeman last week and, taking their cue from some of our Keswick youth activity, their older children decided to film their younger brother Andrew, who's four years old. They sat him in front of a delicious marshmallow, and said that if he could avoid the temptation of eating it for five minutes, he would get a sticker book. He touched the marshmallow, he looked around to distract himself, then looked back at the marshmallow. But he resisted temptation. The sticker book was a better vision, and a more prized goal! And we too have a better vision. Not the tawdry impurity of our world, but the joy of serving a new master, who loves me as fully as a person can be loved; a God who has set me apart to be his.

I am loved by God the Father. I belong to God's holy family. And there is more in the opening verses.

3. I am rescued by God's Son

> Live a life of love, just as Christ loved us and gave himself up for us as a fragrant offering and sacrifice to God. (verse 2)

Again Paul continues his argument from chapter 4 by telling us that Christ's love is a model of the kind of love we are to show. But it's also true that, in our struggle with sin, what Christ has done for us is a wonderful incentive to live for him. Why is that? Well, it's because I have been rescued; I have been purchased by his blood. I am not my own, I've been bought with a price.

How do I overcome the pull of sin? Paul reminded the Galatians of his own testimony: 'the Son of God who loved me and gave himself for me' (Galatians 2:20). And here it is in Ephesians 5:2, 'He gave himself up for us.' It is sacrificial language, of course. 'A fragrant offering' implies the acceptability of Christ's sacrifice. He willingly gave himself as an offering for sin.

I remember reading John White's book, *The Fight*, when he wrote of his longing to live a godly life. He went to conferences, he read books, he longed to change, but he was crushed with a sense of guilt and failure. And then he wrote:

> Light began to break over me when I realized in the depths of my spirit that I was forgiven, cleansed, accepted, justified because of what Christ had done for me. I found I was set free, free to be holy. To my astonishment I discovered that I wanted to live a holy life far more than I wanted to sin. Forgiveness freed me to do what I wanted most.[1]

What have we been rescued from? We are told in verses 5–6:

> For of this you can be sure: no immoral, impure or greedy person – such a person is an idolater – has any inheritance in the kingdom of Christ and of God. Let no one deceive you with empty words, for because of such things God's wrath comes on those who are disobedient.

How are we to understand these verses? After all, at least in our thoughts, many of us commit sexual sins almost every day. First, Paul is describing a lifestyle. This kind of immoral behaviour involves making a deliberate and sustained choice to live in this way. Such a person has given himself up without shame to this way of life. Their lust has become an idolatrous obsession. So those who have given themselves over to immorality, impurity and greed show that they are excluded from eternal life. Such a person is an idolater, says verse 5 – in other words, you have chosen another god. And verse 6 is more severe still: if we live like this, we will be exposed to the wrath of God. But *I am rescued*. Christ gave himself to deliver me from God's wrath. I have a wonderful new future, an inheritance in God's Kingdom. But, at the same time, John Stott was right to say that 'it would be easy for Christians to speed read a paragraph like this, without pausing for reflection, on the assumption that it applies to unbelievers and not to us'.[2] Our assurance of salvation is not an excuse for presumption. Elsewhere Paul urges us not to underestimate our moral obligations, to recognize that we are responsible to Jesus our Judge.

In another powerful piece of writing, 1 Corinthians 6:9–11, Paul again asserts that wrongdoers will not inherit the Kingdom of God. He lists the sexually immoral, adulterers, thieves, slanderers and more. And then he writes in verse 11:

> And that is what some of you were. But you were washed, you were sanctified, you were justified in the name of the Lord Jesus Christ and by the Spirit of our God.

We may feel we have failed God time and time again. How can I go back for forgiveness? Or we feel that we have wandered like some prodigal son into a distant land. Or that worldliness has eaten away at our hearts and it seems impossible to remove it. But 'that is what some of you *were*', Paul said. I am rescued by God's Son. Jesus' sacrifice has been accepted. God's grace is enough. John Newton knew this. As a slave trader, he was truly converted, and he never forgot God's grace to him. And to keep it at the front of his mind, he had a text from Deuteronomy 15:15 written out in bold letters and fastened across the wall in his study: 'Thou shalt remember that thou wast a bondman (slave) in the land of Egypt, and the Lord thy God redeemed thee' (KJV).

So how can I overcome the pull of sin? I must remember what I have been saved from. I am rescued by God's Son.

4. I am thankful for God's grace (verse 4)

As we've seen, Paul has been writing about sexual morality, urging that there must be no place in our conversation for vulgarity, obscenity, or even innuendo. And as we grow up into the family likeness then our attitudes and our conversation change, underpinned by one thing – 'thanksgiving' (verse 4). Sexuality is a subject for thanksgiving, not for joking. We should celebrate all God's good gifts with grateful hearts rather than degrade them with coarse joking.

In fact, this should be our attitude to the whole of life. Thanksgiving means turning our attention away from ourselves towards God; turning towards his grace and his good purposes. In fact, some suggest that thanksgiving is a synonym for the Christian life. It's a mark of the Spirit's work, as Paul says later in verse 20: 'Always giving thanks to God the Father for everything.'

Thankfulness is the exact opposite of self-centredness. It is a recognition of God's generosity. It's a response of gratitude for his saving work – I am thankful for God's gifts, I am thankful that I have been rescued from God's wrath, I am thankful for redeeming, transforming, empowering grace. Grace produces gratitude. The answer to our question – how do I overcome the pull of sin? – lies here too, because it's very difficult to give thanks and to sin at the same time. Thanksgiving is an antidote to the pull of sin.

I am loved; I belong; I am rescued; I am thankful. And here's another motivation to resist sin:

5. I am light in the Lord

Some people see verse 8 as a great summary verse which describes the heartbeat of Ephesians, and perhaps the gospel itself: 'For you were once darkness, but now you are light in the Lord. Live as children of light.'

As we read Ephesians we see Paul constantly making these dramatic contrasts to describe what's happened to us. It's from death to life; from being far away, to being brought near. And here in verse 8 – you've been rescued from the dominion of darkness, and now you are 'light in the Lord'. It's a monumental change of identity. Perhaps this section was used at baptismal services, reminding people that they now have an entirely new nature. And that leads to a different way of living. We're taken out of darkness, and brought into his marvellous light. So now we must live like those who are at home in daylight. We're children of the day. So live in a way that pleases God.

Again the passage gives the contrast: 'Have nothing to do with fruitless deeds of darkness' (verse 11), instead, 'the fruit of the light consists in all goodness, righteousness and truth' (verse 9). The summary is there in verse 10: 'Find out what pleases the Lord.' That's our new orientation as those who are 'light in the Lord'. A fundamental reason for not getting involved in the evil conduct of immoral people is that you are a new person.

For some years I worked with students in Siberia, and always remember the conversion of a man called Jan. He was a Satanist who wanted to turn to Christ. A group of Christians gathered to pray for him. He put his faith in Christ, praying for freedom from his old way of life on the grounds of the cross. And just like the story of Acts 19, they gathered some of the occult objects that linked him to his past. I quote from my friend: 'That night he tore up his book, page after page, and burnt it all, whilst the Christian students sang in Russian, *Jesus is my freedom and my love, he is my salvation*. The next morning it was snowing. The black ashes were covered with a pure white layer, totally covered.' As Birgit wrote, 'Nothing was to be seen of Jan's old life. The old is past, and the new has come.'

Death to life; darkness to light. And did you notice that verse 8 says, 'Now you are light' – our lives and not just our environment have been changed from darkness to light. You are light in union with the Lord. So verse 11 tells us – 'Have nothing to do with the fruitless deeds of darkness, but rather expose them.' Light not only reveals, but it exposes, it penetrates.

A while ago I returned home after a week of travel and, as I stepped in the door, my wife Margaret said, 'Well, do you notice anything different?' And I ran a quick mental checklist: has she had her hair done? Is there a new carpet? She had painted our hallway a light blue, which had refreshed the whole space. But I also noticed that two of the photos on the wall looked grubby. It was actually the new paint which highlighted the faded, dirty edges of the photos. It's like sunlight shining into your dining room, which exposes the dust, the finger marks, the rings from coffee cups. It's like pulling up a rock in your garden – the insects underneath scuttle away. They can't stand the light.

So Christians who truly live a life that pleases God inevitably show up the darkness. And perhaps verse 13 implies that light not only illuminates, it can truly change people: 'Everything that is illuminated becomes a light.' We're not just a mirror, we're a conduit of light. Light that blesses, educates, and restores. We are light-bearers in this dark world. We should ask: to what extent does our life, our family, our local church truly shed the light of Christ in such a world as this?

So how do I overcome the pull of sin? I am loved, I belong, I am rescued, I am thankful, I am light. There's one other thing to say. Don't forget that Paul is writing to the church as a whole. So in seeking to overcome the pull of sin, we should add:

6. I am not alone

Some see these verses as describing Christians who are in danger of backsliding. It's true: our task is to help, exhort and support one another. The fellowship of believers is one where we pray, care and work to help one another keep on track.

The final verse of our section, verse 14, is possibly a quotation from a hymn used at an Easter or a baptismal service: 'Wake up, sleeper, rise from the dead, and Christ will shine on you.' Conversion is waking from sleep, rising from death, being brought out of darkness into light. And the light that shines on believers is the empowering presence of the Lord. He enables us to turn from sin and live a life of holiness. We are not alone: we have the fellowship of believers and the empowering presence of the Spirit of Christ.

There's no question that we face a daily struggle with sin. We feel its pull all the time. We experience the heat of the spiritual battle. So let's remember what we have seen in this passage. This is God's work. It is the Father who loves us, the Son who rescues us, the Spirit who empowers us. He takes us as we are, and he sets to work in making us what we should be. God himself enables us to resist the pull of sin.

Notes

1. John White, *The Fight* (IVP, 2008).
2. John Stott, *The Message of the Ephesians* (BST) (IVP, 1991), p. 198.

What Does It Mean to Be Filled with the Spirit?

by Ray Evans

Ray Evans has led Grace Community Church, Bedford, for over thirty years. He is a popular speaker at UK conferences, theological colleges and church weekends. He jointly wrote *Learning to Lead* (FIEC), and his latest book is *Ready, Steady, Grow* (IVP). He is married to Jenny, and they have four grown-up children and four grandchildren. Earlier in life, he did two geography degrees at Cambridge. He is a passionate sportsman, a keen Arsenal supporter, and loves reading.

What Does It Mean to Be Filled with the Spirit? Ephesians 5:15–21

Do you see the heading of this passage? 'Be very careful, then, how you live' (verse 15). This passage is to do with the whole of you and the whole of your life. The apostle doesn't want you to waste your one and only life, he doesn't want you to muddle through it or wreck it. So he is going to tell you how to make your life count. And you'll see that there are three things he says, three areas where he says: 'Listen to me.' The one we are homing in on this evening is in verse 18, 'Do not get drunk on wine which leads to debauchery. Instead, be filled with the Spirit.'

Now this doesn't mean it's okay if I get drunk on beer, cider or spirits! Before we proceed we need to face up to this serious issue. It is reckoned that it costs twenty-one billion pounds a year to deal with the problems associated with drunkenness. To put that in perspective, the *total* annual NHS budget is over a hundred billion pounds. So, it is a huge cost to our society, but of course it's really about individuals isn't it? Of those who do drink, the statistics tell us that 52% of men and 53% of women drink more than is healthy for them. Many younger Christians wonder if it really matters, if drinking too much is really that important. Well, here the apostle is very clear. If we want to please the Holy Spirit, if we want to be obedient to our Lord Jesus and do the will of our Father in heaven, don't get drunk on wine. There are no exceptions you see.

Now some people have argued that being filled with the Spirit is a bit like being filled with spirits; we become overwhelmed and out of control. Well, just so we know, that's not the proper application. Paul gives us here, not three comparisons of similarity, but three contrasts of opposites. 'Do not get drunk on wine . . . instead be filled with the Spirit'. Notice the other two contrasts. First in verses 15–16, 'Not as unwise but as wise, making the most of every opportunity because the days are evil.' What is he saying? He is saying, 'I am being realistic of life. There are real evils all around you. As a Christian believer I want you to make good choices. You are going to have opportunities to follow the Lord Jesus or give into evil. Don't be unwise but wise; making good, right, best choices that will impact your life.'

Notice the second contrast in verse 17, 'Do not be foolish but understand what the Lord's will is.' He's dealing with one of those things that we easily fall into – head versus heart. Or, to put it like this, some Christians are 'Word' Christians and some are 'Spirit' Christians. Some people are very cerebral, others very intuitive and passionate. Perhaps some read this section and think, 'This is more me – the Spirit, feeling, passion and excitement.' Well, Paul won't let us do that. In the parallel passage in Colossians 3:16 Paul uses almost identical words, about speaking to one another and singing: 'Let the message of Christ dwell in you richly.' There is no conflict between Word and Spirit. The Spirit makes the Word alive, the Spirit make our hearts grow warmer as we hear the Word. There is no feeling versus intellect conflict.

So there are three contrasts we need to understand that lead us to the big command in this passage: Be filled with the Spirit. Now there is a lot to unpack here, our time is limited. So to help us I'm going to work through four 'C's. And the first one is that it is a 'command'. 'Be filled' is in the imperative, it is an 'ought to', 'should', a 'must'. It is a command to Christians, not an optional extra.

The second 'C' is 'corporate'. 'Be filled . . .' is in the plural. It's 'you' plural. He's thinking of each and every one. He's going to go on and say, verse 19, 'speaking to one another'. He's not saying, 'You Spirit-filled lot talk to this group over here because they are a bit slow.' He is speaking to all Christians. Together, corporately, he wants us to be filled with the Holy Spirit of God. Now immediately you see he is not talking about an elite or special group of Christians who are full of the Spirit.

My father was in the air force for thirty-seven years and at one time we moved to Catterick in North Yorkshire. My brother's best friend's brother and his dad were both in the

SAS. The SAS is the envy of the world and their selection procedure, the Special Forces Aptitude Test, lasts five gruelling months. People have been killed on this training, as you may know from the news. It has a 90% failure rate. The men and women who get through, to quote *Men in Black*, are, 'the best of the best of the best.' Now what Paul is saying here is not that some Christians – the best of the best of the best, the select elect, those special few, the really holy ones – are filled with the Spirit and the rest of us just have to rock on as we are. No, he is saying to all Christians: God wants all his children to be filled by the Holy Spirit, it's corporate.

The third 'C' is continuous; it's not a one-off thing. 'Be filled' is in the present continuous tense, it means go on being filled with the Holy Spirit of God. Paul is not talking about a crisis – 'I was going on in my Christian life then I had a crisis and got filled with the Holy Spirit and everything changed.' Now we can have very special experiences. Indeed, the apostle Paul said, 'I know a man in Christ who . . . was caught up to the third heaven' (2 Corinthians 12:2). We are not playing down our special experiences of God's grace and mercy, but this passage is about being filled with the Holy Spirit, present continuous.

Let me explain. A few years ago my wife and our four children went to France for the very first time. I was as nervous as you like. I memorized a phrase, *le plein, s'il vous plaît*, which means, 'Fill it up, please.' I'd reckoned that as long as we've got fuel in the car, I could at least get home. So we travelled across on the ferry, we drove down to

Normandy, and I was getting nervous as the petrol lights were beginning to flash. I found this petrol station and I used the magic words, and it worked! I couldn't believe it! French actually works! So the car was filled up and I was good for another 500 miles.

Now, that is not what Paul has in mind here. He is not saying, 'Get filled up and see how far you can go. And, before the lights begin to blink and the car comes to a crunch on the side of an autoroute in France, you better fill up again.' No! Too many of us think like that. We think, 'If I get an injection of the Holy Spirit at Keswick it will get me through until Christmas, and then maybe at church I'll get another bit to last me until Easter, and then I'll get back to Keswick where I'll get it again.' That is not what Paul's got in mind when he says, 'Be filled with the Holy Spirit.' It's like breathing; if you are alive you are breathing. Being filled with the Spirit is how a Christian lives. Go on being filled by the Spirit.

And the fourth 'C' is that it is 'caused' to you, it's in the passive. That means you don't fill yourself up, God fills you. In one sense God commands what he will do to you. 'Be filled, all of you, go on being filled, by me. I want that in your lives.'

So as we think of those four 'C's it leaves us all with a choice. For unless we are filled by God with his Spirit what are we full of? We are full of ourselves and it's not attractive is it? Even when we do spiritual things we can be full of ourselves – we need to be noticed, thanked, admired. But this marvellous passage gives us an alternative. We can be full of God and full of Jesus Christ by the power of the Holy Spirit. Turn back over to Ephesians 3:14–17, what does the apostle say?

> For this reason I kneel before the Father, from whom every family in heaven and on earth derives its name. I pray that out of his glorious riches he may strengthen you in power through his Spirit in your inner being, so that Christ may dwell in your heart through faith.

The power of the Spirit is to bring you to believe in Jesus and keep on believing in Jesus. Then Paul goes on, verses 17–19:

> I pray that you, being rooted and established in love, may have power together with all the Lord's holy people to grasp how wide and long and high and deep is the love of Christ, and to know this love that surpasses knowledge – that you may be filled to the measure of all the fullness of God.

We tend to think, 'I want to be filled with the Holy Spirit.' The text is saying that the Holy Spirit is the one who fills you. When you are filled by the Holy Spirit you are full of Christ. And when you are full of Christ, you are close to the Father. The Holy Spirit's role is to point you to Christ and keep showing you that Christ has dealt with your sins on the cross, the Father is completely reconciled, and the judgment that your sins deserve has gone for ever! The

Holy Spirit wants to show you the sufficiency of the person and the work of Jesus, to keep you looking to him and trusting in him. You go on believing because the Holy Spirit is yours, you are being filled by him to look to Jesus. That helps us understand how we get filled.

Now this text tells us to be filled, it doesn't tell us how, but there is another passage that does, Galatians 3:1–3:

> You foolish Galatians! Who has bewitched you? Before your very eyes Jesus Christ was clearly portrayed as crucified. I would like to learn just one thing from you: did you receive the Spirit by the works of the law or by believing what you heard? Are you so foolish? After beginning by means of the Spirit, are you now trying to finish by means of the flesh?

How did they receive the Holy Spirit? They heard the message of Christ crucified for their sins. They believed and as they looked to Christ, they received the Spirit. And that's how you go on receiving the Spirit, you look to Christ.

That great Victorian preacher, Charles Spurgeon, became a Christian when he heard these words 'Look unto me and be ye saved, all the ends of the earth' (Isaiah 45:22, KJV). The preacher told him, 'You have nothin' to do but to look and live.'[1] He looked and he lived. But he kept on looking, and he kept on living. People quote Spurgeon as saying this, which I think is profoundly helpful: 'I looked to Christ and the dove of the Holy Spirit flew into my heart, and when I looked into my heart to see if he was there, he flew away again.' Do you see that? That's exactly what Paul is saying here in Ephesians. Be filled by the Spirit so that you look to Christ. You receive the Spirit by believing in Jesus, you go on believing, your faith in Christ deepens, your sense of assurance that the cross has done it all gives you peace with God, it brings you close to God, so that we come before the eternal throne and cry 'Abba Father'. That's the work of the Spirit, applying the work of Christ to our hearts. So if we want more of the work of the Holy Spirit, so that we become like Jesus, we keep looking to Jesus.

Maybe some of us have been full of ourselves for too long. Maybe tonight is the time just to be quiet in your heart, even as I speak, and say 'Heavenly Father, forgive me that I have not been living by your Spirit, looking to my Saviour, trusting in his merits and following him. I've been living my own way for my own purposes with me at the centre. I am sorry, will you forgive me?' Tonight, why don't you make that choice to put self on the cross and Christ on the throne once more in your life?

But it doesn't end there, being filled by the Spirit will have consequences in your life. You see, after the command 'Be filled by the Spirit' there are five participles. You see in verse 19, 'Be filled by the Spirit, addressing one another in psalms, hymns and spiritual songs, singing and making melody to the Lord in your heart', then verse 20, 'giving thanks' and finally, in verse 21, 'submitting' (ESV). The participles may not be clear in your version but they are there. And all those participles hang on the 'Be filled by the Spirit' command. They flow from a Christian who is being filled by the Spirit, who is looking to Christ and close to the Father.

Now I just want to look at them for a few seconds really. I want to start in reverse order, verse 21, 'submitting'. A Christian filled by the Spirit, close to the Father, will be a meek person, willing to put themselves out for others' benefit. The context Paul is talking about is the home and work. Being filled with and by the Spirit is not something churchy, religious or that just happens in a worship service; it is all of life. So wives are going to submit to a husband's loving leadership; Christian children are going to obey their parents; slaves are going to work honestly for their masters. It outworks itself in everyday life. *Fruitfulness on the Frontline*, as Mark Greene describes it.[2]

Next, 'giving thanks to God'. Notice the lovely Trinitarian structure: by the Spirit we give thanks to the Father through Christ our Lord in everything, always. Gratitude becomes part of who I am. I become a grateful person. Grateful for life, breath, music, friends, church, and all God's benefits. See the contrast with how we were before we became Christians: 'Although they knew God they neither glorified him as God nor gave thanks to him' (Romans 1:21). So, let me ask you, 'Are you a grateful person? Does gratitude characterize your life?' Well, if the Spirit is at work in your life, if you are asking the Spirit to reveal more and more of Jesus to you, that's what you will become.

I want to close by looking at the three participles to do with singing (verse 19). It's interesting that the Holy Spirit's work in us leads us to sing. It is said that there are more choirs in Britain than fish and chip shops. Singing has become very fashionable. And people are discovering there is something about singing that touches us at the core of our being.

Let me tell you a story about the power of singing. It is about a lady called Karen. She found out she was having another baby and did what she could to help her three-year-old son Michael prepare for the new sibling. They found out the new baby was going to be a girl and day after day, night after night, Michael would sing to his sister in his mummy's tummy. The pregnancy progresses normally for Karen, but then the labour pains come, every five minutes, every minute. Complications arise during delivery and a caesarean section is required.

Finally, Michael's little sister is born but she's in a serious condition. With a siren howling in the night, she is transferred to another hospital, to a neonatal intensive care unit. The days inch by, the little girl gets worse, the paediatric specialist tells the parents there is very little hope and to be prepared for the worst. Karen and her husband contact a local cemetery about a burial plot. They had fixed up a special room in their house for the new baby, now they are planning a funeral.

Michael keeps begging his parents to let him see his sister. 'I want to sing to her,' he says. Week two, still in intensive care. It looks as if a funeral will come before the week is over. Michael keeps nagging about singing to his sister, but kids are not allowed in ICU. Well, Karen works out that if he doesn't see his sister now he may never see her alive. So she dresses him up in an oversized scrubs suit and marches him into ICU. He looks like a walking laundry basket. The head nurse recognizes him as a child and bellows, 'Get that kid out of here now. No children allowed in ICU!' But the mother in Karen rises up strong, and this usually mild lady stared steely eyed into the head nurse's face. Her lips are firm, he is not leaving until he sings to his sister. Karen tows Michael to his sister's bedside. He gazes at the tiny infant losing the battle to live and he begins to sing. In the pure-hearted voice of a three-year-old, he sings, 'You are my sunshine'.[3] Instantly the baby girl responds, her pulse rate becomes calm and steady. The ragged, strained breathing becomes as smooth as a kitten's purr. Michael's little sister relaxes as healing rest seems to sweep over her. The next day, the very next day, the little girl is well enough to go home. The medical staff just called it a miracle, but Karen called it a miracle of God's love.

Now, if God can take the song of a three-year-old to bring life physically to a dying child, can he not take the songs of his people when they worship him, to bring life to those who are not yet alive to him? Well, the apostle Paul says he can. Paul says when unbelievers come among you and hear the Words of God, 'the secrets of their hearts are laid bare. So they will fall down and worship God, exclaiming, "God is really among you!"' (1 Corinthians 14:24–25). That's what we long for in our churches isn't it?

And what we begin now will go on for ever, it will be taken up in a far more amazing song in heaven: 'And then I heard every creature in heaven,' and your voice and my voice will be there, singing, 'To him who sits on the throne and to the Lamb be praise and honour and glory and power, for ever and ever!' (Revelation 5:13).

Do you know that old spiritual song, 'When the saints go marching in . . . I want to be in that number'? How do you know you are going to be in that number? Because you start singing by the Spirit *now*, you look to Christ, you receive the grace of God in Christ, the Spirit is at work in your life, you know you are at peace with God, you love the God that died for your sins on the cross, you have come to know the giving, self-sacrificing Father and you want to start singing – that's the fruit of the Spirit in our lives. May God enable each one of us to say, 'O God, point me to Christ again. Fill me by your Spirit with love for my Saviour who loved me and gave himself for me.' And then, let's sing to God's praise. Amen.

Notes

1. W. Y. Fullerton, *Charles Spurgeon: A Biography: The Life of C. H. Spurgeon by a Close Friend* (CreateSpace Independent Publishing Platform, 2014), p. 22.
2. Mark Greene, *Fruitfulness on the Frontline* (IVP, 2014).
3. 'You are my sunshine', recorded by Jimmie Davis and Charles Mitchell in 1939.

What Kind of Life Does God Use in His Mission?

by Calisto Odede

Calisto Odede is Senior Pastor of Nairobi Pentecostal Church. He worked with the Fellowship of Christian Unions (FOCUS) for thirteen years, and then served with the International Fellowship of Evangelical Students (IFES) for eight years. Calisto has travelled to many countries conducting Bible exposition and leadership training. He has been a featured speaker at numerous conferences and mission conventions, including being an expositor at the Lausanne III Congress, Cape Town, in 2010. Calisto and his wife, Elizabeth, have three sons: Victor, Benson and Michael.

What Kind of Life Does God Use in His Mission? Ephesians 6:10–20

I'm sure it has been a great week for each and every one of us and it is unfortunate that it is coming to an end tomorrow evening. But we do pray that it is only the Convention that is coming to an end and that the work of God is beginning. We are going out afresh on a mission as the Convention ends. Tonight we turn to a particularly familiar passage of Scripture from Ephesians 6:10–20. We are looking at the question, what kind of life does God use in his mission?

A man of European origin was brought to me by his wife. She was concerned that he wasn't sleeping. The reason he wasn't sleeping was because in the middle of the night he appeared to be having a fight or an engagement with an unknown entity. After talking with him he mentioned that he had been involved with some Eastern religion leading deep into Chinese tai chi and, as a result of that, he could do some things that were quite abnormal. I got up from my seat and went round to where he was sitting. The moment I put out my hands to pray over him it was as if I had touched him with 240 volts of electricity. Something knocked him down, he began to writhe on the floor like a snake; the man had a spirit inside of him. You see, brothers and sisters, the world in which you and I live is not the only world in existence. Beyond what we can see, smell, taste and touch is another world that is just as real as the world that you and I are operating in on a day-by-day basis. John Milton wrote in the seventeenth century:

> Millions of spiritual creatures walk the earth
> Unseen, both when we wake, and when we sleep.[1]

You cannot detect them by X-ray, radar, ultrasound, scanners or any gadgets that modern day science uses, but that does not mean that they are not there. Now there are two dangers that we certainly need to avoid. One of the dangers is developing a rationalistic, materialistic kind of mind-set. This worldview dismisses the spirit world and believes heathen and civilized pagans should be weaned from their uncultured views, as everything is explicable in terms of scientific rationalization. On the other hand, there is an animistic view, where a force is attributed to every object. So we begin to see demons everywhere – in trees, mountains, rivers, waters, oceans.

We need to be aware that this world exists. But you cannot live on our planet, whether you are watching children's cartoons or Harry Potter, without being aware that there is an over-fascination with demons. I think C. S. Lewis balances it correctly when he says:

> There are two equal and opposite errors into which our race can fall about the devils. One is to disbelieve in their existence. The other is to believe, and to feel an excessive and unhealthy interest in them. They themselves are equally pleased by both errors and hail a materialist or a magician with the same delight.[2]

Now the passage before us has been often used to propagate and to preach issues touching on spiritual warfare. That's not our subject tonight. Paul has looked at the life of the Ephesians and emphasized the importance of developing Christian character qualities. He points out to us how we can walk the Christian journey and become more and more Christlike. In chapter 5 Paul goes into what is popularly considered the 'household codes'. He picks some words and terms that are regularly used and gives them a Christian connotation. So in Paul's view family and marriage is a mission; it is a mission to the extent that it is comparable with what Christ Jesus did when he left glory and came to our planet. Marriage is a mission. So it's not 'What can I get out of it?' but 'What can I give into it?' He talks of the family; that domesticity and parenting is a mission. He talks about the responsibility of children, it's a mission. He talks about work relationships in the market place. Whether we are dealing with servants, slaves or people that are working with us or for us, it is a mission. And so it is important for none of us to feel, 'I am not a missionary therefore the subject of mission doesn't interest me at all.' Living in engagement with what God wants us to do is actually a mission! And so in this latter part of this letter, after painting for us the heavenly scene where we are lifted up and are seated high with Christ Jesus in the heavenly places, Paul now turns to the believers and says, 'Now get ready, you are in a war.'

We are reminded of the words of the movie *Mission Impossible*: 'Good evening Mr Briggs, your mission should you choose to accept it . . .' And Paul turns to the Ephesians and says, 'You have a mission, you are in a war. You are not a civilian. Do not behave as if you didn't have enemies.' You are actually engaged in a battle. And you may wonder how did I get myself here? The moment you made a commitment to the Lord Jesus Christ as your personal Saviour the forces that we have talked about began targeting you as an object of their attack. You enlisted in the military and the Lord Jesus Christ.

And so he picks up this spiritual warfare motive and uses it, not to intimate or threaten the Christians, but to encourage them so that they would be able to stand. And in this portion of Scripture three times he talks about standing: in verse 13, Paul says 'stand your ground', again in verse 13, 'after you have done everything to stand' and in verse 14 he says, 'stand firm then'. In other words, Paul is saying that the encouragement that he is giving here is not that we may turn and flee but that we may be able to stand in spite of the warfare in which we are engaged. His purpose is that although there are enemies that rage against us we may withstand the onslaught, come out victorious and advance the kingdom of God. And so who are these people that God uses? What kind of individuals are they?

First of all there are those who are plugged into the sources of God's power. Verse 10, 'Finally, be strong in the Lord and in his mighty power.' He has been talking with the Ephesians for five chapters and now he says at the close of his address, 'The final thing that I am mentioning to you, is that you may be strong.' In other words, Paul says, 'In conclusion, be strong.' To be strong does not mean get yourself some grit and then come out as strong. It simply means allow yourself to be strengthened in the Lord and by the power of God. And the kind of power that he is referring to, the strength of his might, is the highest it could ever be. The greatest power of God is available to strengthen you. Paul says, therefore, plug into the resources of the power of God so that you may be strengthened. He himself knew what he was talking about. Isn't it Paul who wrote, 'God's power is made perfect in weakness . . . that is why, for Christ's sake I delight in weakness . . . for when I am weak, then I am strong' (2 Corinthians 12:9–10)? And so Paul had learnt how to draw from the strength that comes from the Lord and he turns to the Ephesians and says, 'What I have learnt for myself I want to recommend to you, plug in to God's strength. Draw from God's ability and God's unique strength for yourself.' It is only when we are strong in the Lord that we can be able to stand, not in our own strength but in the strength that the Lord gives.

So when you seem to be overwhelmed by temptations, be strong. When you are on the verge of giving up, be strong. When the attack seems so vicious, be strong. When fear seems to assail you, be strong. When it seems like you are weak and struggling, be strong. And the strength is simply plugging in to the resources of God's power. I saw a cartoon the other day of a man sitting down next to a television set. The television set had been taken apart completely, it was in pieces. The man was sitting there with his tools next to him and the caption read, 'The problem may not be as difficult as you think.' What was the problem? The plug was hanging outside the socket. He had not plugged in, that is why his TV was not working. And God is inviting us, not to run the Christian life with our own strength, but to plug into the strength that God provides. When we plug into his strength it begins to flow through us so that we are able to stand.

Secondly, Paul says God uses those who are clothed with God's armour, verses 11–17. He points out, verse 11, 'Put on the full armour of God, so that you can take your stand against the devil's schemes.' The word he uses here means the systematic and methodological trickery of evil presided over by the devil. In other words, we are dealing with an enemy that is putting certain systems in place in order to trick us. Those who circumvent the ways of the evil one must learn that we are dealing with an enemy that is out to trick us. He uses the word 'struggle' or 'wrestle', verse 12. Wrestle is close combat, it's face-to-face, hand-to-hand, foot-to-foot or perhaps teeth-to-teeth. And he says, 'our struggle is not against flesh and blood', in other words, we are not wrestling against those we consider our enemies but against a hierarchy of evil. Fallen spirits and angels, invisible and unseen rulers, lie behind all that is happening to us. Spiritual beings of wickedness are in the heavenly places. The great threats we face are not physical ones. The greatest challenge is actually spiritual; forces of evil which will try to knock us down. Charles Hodge writes:

> If Satan is really the prince of the power of darkness, ruler and god of this world, if he is author of physical and moral evil, the great enemy of God, of Christ and his people, full of cunning and malice, if he is constantly seeking whom we may destroy, seducing people into sin, blinding their minds and suggesting evil and sceptical thoughts. If all this is true, then to be ignorant of it, or to deny it, or to enter into this conflict as though it were merely a struggle between the good and the bad principles in our own heart is to rush blindfold to destruction.[3]

Now, it is encouraging to know that Christ has triumphed over these powers. So although we are being invited to put on the armour of God that we may be able to withstand, we already know that our enemy is defeated. Colossians 2: 14–15 records that Christ has triumphed over powers, principalities, rulers, and authorities, on the cross. On the cross he disarmed them and he made a public show of them. So we are fighting a battle whose end we already know because Satan is defeated.

A number of years ago in an office where I used to work, we had a cobra visit us. A lady saw the cobra and screamed. We jumped up and killed this snake. The surprising thing was that even after we had killed it the tail was wagging. The cobra was completely harmless but the tail was still wagging. And that is exactly what has happened to the devil. He has been crushed and defeated by Jesus and what we are fighting now is basically the wagging tail.

And so we are invited therefore, if we are going to engage in God's mission, to put on the whole armour of God. And what is this armour he is talking about? The belt of truth: truth not only as theological and doctrinal sound beliefs, orthodoxy; but also orthopraxy, truth in terms of an individual's life, their sincerity and integrity. Put on the belt of truth!

Paul is writing this letter in jail. This is one of the prison letters, and outside the jail, or standing by, guarding him, is a Roman soldier. And as he looks at this soldier he starts picking up, piece-by-piece, the attire that the soldier is wearing and he turns it into a spiritual element. So Paul looks at the belt that they used to hold their clothes up so that they would not trip or so their clothes would not fall apart. And he says that belt is the truth, hold on to the truth based on God's Word. Truth does not allow us to cover up. Have the truth on in your life.

Secondly, the breastplate of righteousness. God considers us righteousness, not because of what we have done, but because of what Christ Jesus has done for us on the cross. 'God made him who had no sin to be sin for us, so that we might become the righteousness of God' (2 Corinthians 5:21). Christ is our righteousness. Put on the righteousness of God, not your own righteousness, which is like filthy rags in the eyes of God.

Thirdly, the readiness of the gospel on the foot. You could view this image in two ways. One, so that you may be stable and not slip you need shoes. The shoes that you need to wear are the gospel. Secondly, go back to the words of the prophet Isaiah, 'how beautiful are the feet of those who bring good news'. This image could be being used to say that when you take the good news you are putting on the readiness of the gospel; you are ready to share it out.

Next is the shield of faith to deflect the fiery darts and arrows that the enemy is firing. I grew up in a village where we used to have tribal wars and we all knew how to use a shield. The strongest shield was actually made of hippo skin. You would use that to deflect any arrows that were thrown at you. Paul says, 'Use the shield of faith. Use the faith that justifies you before God to deflect any attack that the evil one throws at you.'

The helmet of salvation is a protection for the head, for the mind, as you put it over your head. The sword of the

Spirit, an offensive weapon that you would use not only to defend but to attack, is basically the Word of the living God. Paul says, 'If you are going to go out on a mission and want to be engaged in serving the Lord effectively, put on all these, dress in these.'

He doesn't end there. Paul says the person who would be used of God is one who is engaged in prayer (verse 18). Although Paul does not give prayer an equivalent attire, he sees it as part and parcel of all this Christian element that would enable you to stand. To pray in the Spirit is to pray a prayer that is energized by the Spirit of God. 'We do not know what we ought to pray for, but the Spirit himself intercedes for us through wordless groans' (Romans 8:26). This is prayer inspired by the Spirit. It may include praying in tongues but should not be limited to that; it is Spirit-energized prayer. Pray with thanksgiving, petitions, requests, and intercessions; pray mentally, vocally, individually and corporately; fast, hold all-night prayer vigils – all this is included when Paul says pray, 'with all kinds of prayer and request' (verse 18). The people God wants to use in his mission field are people of prayer.

Finally, they ought to be people who are burdened about the world. In verses 19–20 Paul says:

> Pray also for me, that whenever I speak, words may be given to me so that I will fearlessly make known the mystery of the gospel, for which I am an ambassador in chains. Pray that I may declare it fearlessly, as I should.

Although Paul had written close to half of the New Testament, he is asking for prayers. Although he has preached throughout the then-known world and seen cities turned upside down, he is asking for prayers. Although he had raised a dead man, he is asking for prayers. Although he had cast out demons all over the place, he is asking for prayers. Although he had gone up to the third heaven and heard things that human beings are not allowed to hear, he is asking for prayers. Sometimes we become too self-sufficient in our missions and ministries. We focus on our problems and stigmatize our prayers believing if you need prayer then you are using a crutch.

Paul turns and says, 'Pray also for me' (verse 19). What should you pray for? Three things. Firstly, pray that my preaching would be energized by God as I declare his Word. Secondly, pray for fearless proclamation to make known with boldness the mystery of Christ. Pray that as I stand before the people I will not be shy. Thirdly, pray for me that I would be an ambassador of Christ, a messenger of Christ, even one who is a prisoner at the time of writing.

If we are to be used of the Lord, we need to ask God to move in our hearts, that the things that burn in the heart of God – those who have not heard the gospel, those who have not been reached, the preaching of the Word of God – would burn in our hearts too, that we too would become part and parcel of what God is doing across the world. There are many of us who are just concerned about ourselves and not about neighbours, friends, or family.

On the plane coming here, I sat next to an Asian who turned out to have a Buddhist background. Someone had been witnessing to him in this country for quite a while. He saw me reading a Christian book and said, 'Someone had told me to read some portions of the Bible but I have problems with the proof of God's existence.' Over the next thirty minutes that young man gave his heart to the Lord Jesus Christ, and I prayed for him on the plane. You see, God calls us not because we are strong, we may be weak, we may be facing a great enemy, but he calls us that we may just be available to him. You may feel like a wounded soldier but don't leave the fight. Stand in the battle, put your armour on, and be strengthened by God's power. You are loved and accepted; stand and be available to him.

Notes

1. John Milton, *Paradise Lost* (1667; 1674), Book IV, line 678.
2. C. S. Lewis, *The Screwtape Letters: Letters from a Senior to a Junior Devil* (William Collins, 2016).
3. Charles Hodge, *Ephesians (Crossway Classic Commentary)* (IVP, 1984), p. 189.

How Can I Keep Going?

by Bill Bygroves

Bill Bygroves has been the Pastor at Bridge Chapel in Liverpool for thirty-five years. He also serves as the Chaplain at Liverpool Football Club. He has been married to Dot for over forty years, they have four grown-up children and three adorable grandchildren.

How Can I Keep Going?
Ephesians 3:14–21

How can I keep going? Number one, be empowered. Number two, be established. Number three, be encouraged.

He was a man of history and destiny. The man of his hour. Born in aristocracy, raised in prosperity, with the looks of a celebrity and destined for world supremacy. At the age of twenty he was king of his country. At the age of thirty, he was king of the world. He conquered two worlds, east and west, and brought all the spoils of war with him: all the riches of Greece, all the treasures of Egypt, all the gold of Babylon, all the abundance of Asia, all the prizes of Persia. His name was Alexander, they call him 'The Great'. And people worshipped him. However, in his early thirties he sat down and wept as a dejected man because there were no more worlds left to conquer. He ruined his life with drink and excess. He died of fever in his bed and he left specific instructions concerning his funeral. His hands were to be unclenched and uncovered. It was to be a testimony to the world of the emptiness of power and of the poverty of his own soul.

I remind you, not all that glitters is gold. Alexander – along with millions, including many in our day and generation, where leisure, pleasure and treasure are the gods of the age – found out that money will buy you anything, except happiness. Money will take you anywhere, except heaven. I'll remind you that power is a delusion; it is the chasing after the wind. But I'll remind you that you are a child of God: born again of the Spirit of God, indwelt by the Spirit of God, his Spirit bearing witness with your spirit, assuring you that you are a child of God. You need to remember the worlds of that old African blasphemer, who became a wonderful Christian, John Newton:

> Fading is the worldling's pleasure,
> All his boasted pomp and show.
> Solid joys and lasting treasures,
> None but Zion's children know.'[1]

If you are a child of God, I remind you, you are rich indeed: maybe not financially, maybe not physically, maybe not circumstantially, but spiritually. I remind you what we have learnt this week – you and I are blessed with every spiritual blessing in heavenly places in Christ Jesus. God, in the Trinity of his persons, in the councils of eternity past, set his love upon you. He chose you. His Son agreed to come in time to live the life you could never have lived, to die the death you deserved to die, to rise again for your justification, and to become your great high priest. The Holy Spirit agreed in time past that he would open your eyes, unstop your ears, quicken your heart, and bring you from darkness to life, from the power of Satan unto God. I remind you, if you are in Christ, regardless of how you feel, regardless of how you have failed, you are the apple of his eye, you are the treasure of his heart, you are the object of his love, and you are the subject of his grace from all eternity to all eternity. And the apostle Paul, writing from a prison cell in Rome, writing to the Ephesians, not just with the Spirit of power but the Spirit of prophecy, will know that men and women in their millions and billions will be blessed by him putting pen to paper, writing about the spiritual blessings which are ours in Christ Jesus.

He writes this epistle chained to a Roman soldier. I remind you, he is not just teaching, but he is praying. Twice in this epistle we find the apostle Paul in prayer. This is sacred Scripture. If I could, I would say to you, 'We need to take the shoes off our feet, for the ground upon which we stand is holy ground.' Here is the beloved apostle Paul, chained to a Roman guard, he goes to his knees, and he prays for the Ephesian Christians, and he prays for you and for me.

'Father,' he prays, 'may your people be empowered.' 'Father,' he prays, 'may your people be established.' 'Father,' he prays, 'may your people be encouraged.' 'For this reason,' verse 14, 'I kneel before the Father from whom every family in heaven and on earth derives its name.'

> No earthly father loves like thee,
> No mother, e'er so mild,
> Bears and forbears as thou hast done
> With me thy sinful child.[2]

Paul is saying something like, 'The whole family of the redeemed bears your name, we are part of your family, you are our Father in heaven. And I pray for these Ephesians Christians that they would be empowered.' He says, verses 16–17, 'I pray that out of his glorious riches he may strengthen you with power, through his Spirit in your inner being, so that Christ may dwell in your hearts through faith.' 'Father, would you make your people inwardly strong, spiritually strong, richer, deeper, stronger, on the inside.'

I was with the young people last night. I told them I was getting a bit older, but they still wanted me to dance. One thing is for sure, if you are getting older, you know that it is very true what is written on a clock in Chester Cathedral:

> When as a child I laughed and wept,
> Time crept.
> When as a youth, I dreamt and talked,
> Time walked.
> When I became a full-grown man
> Time ran.

When older still I daily grew
Time flew.
Soon I shall find as travelling on –
Time gone.

If all your focus is on the outward and the physical, you and I are going to be very disappointed, that is for sure. And when some of you young people go into Topman and they tell you what you really need to do is to look after the outward, or ladies when you go into Next and you are told what you really need to do is look elegant, sophisticated and beautiful, there is nothing wrong with that. But I want to tell you, more important, far more important, is your inner being, your inner man. The apostle Paul will write in 2 Corinthians 4:16: 'outwardly we are wasting away, yet inwardly we are being renewed day by day.'

Paul's prayer to God for the Ephesians is: 'I want your *dunamis*, I want that power, that mighty irresistible power of God the Holy Spirit, of the Spirit of our Lord Jesus Christ, to strengthen the inner being, the inner man, so that Christ may dwell in your hearts through faith.' What a wonderful word 'dwell' is! It means that Christ might live, might abide, might not be viewed as a visitor or an outsider, but be welcome.

I grew up in a rough part of Liverpool. Every Wednesday was Bally Ann day. Bally Ann day was the day that you had no money. And your mother would send you to the shop to get some meat on tick, some bacon and eggs on tick. I would be embarrassed but I'd come home, walk in the parlour and on the wall would be written these words: 'Christ is the head of this house. The unseen guest at every meal, the silent listener to every conversation.' O that Christ would dwell in our spiritual houses: that he would come into our minds, come into our wills, come into our affections, come into our emotions, come into our choices, come into our relationships.

Some of you remember the days when you had no refrigerators. Some of you can remember when all the dirty washing went in the cubby hole. When someone important knocked on the door your mother would quickly put all her dirty washing in the cubby hole. The problem with that was the outside of the rooms looked tidy, but there was a strange smell. No! Clean up your life by allowing Christ to fill every part. May you be empowered by God the Holy Spirit in your inner being so that Christ can be a visitor, not just a visitor, an abider, not just an abider, a friend – someone who lives within you. Don't you love that hymn:

May the mind of Christ my Saviour
Live in me from day to day,
By his love and power controlling
All I do or say.

May the Word of God dwell richly,
In my heart from hour to hour,
So that all may see I triumph
Only through his power.

May the peace of God my Father
Rule my life in everything,
That I may be calm to comfort
Sick and sorrowing.

May the love of Jesus fill me,
As the waters fill the sea;
Him exalting, self-abasing –
This is victory.

May I run the race before me,
Strong and brave to face the foe,
Looking only unto Jesus
As I onward go.[3]

Friends, be empowered by the Holy Spirit and let Christ dwell in every corner of your heart by faith.

Number two, 'Father, establish your people.' Friends, be established. Verses 17–19,

> And I pray that you, being rooted and established in love, may have power, together with all the Lord's holy people, to grasp how wide and long and high and deep is the love of Christ, and to know this love that surpasses knowledge – that you may be filled to the measure of all the fullness of God.

Friends at Keswick, will you be established? I love the words that are used here. 'Rooted' – that is a good word, isn't it?

It is an agricultural word; dig deep, dig your roots down deep. In July 2014 as a result of some DNA testing the oldest tree in Britain was discovered. It was in Saint Cynog's churchyard in Powys in Wales. It is 5,000 years old. Think about that for a minute. Have you ever been to Wales? It is a bit like Scotland and the Lake District. Every time I go there, it rains! However, think about this tree. The wind has howled against it, the storms have come, the lightning has flashed, and the thunder has clapped. Anything and everything that has been coming against this tree it has withstood. It has withstood every trial and every storm because its roots are deep. Paul prays that you be 'rooted', that you would deepen your roots in Christ.

He prays too that we would be 'established'. That's an architectural word, isn't it? It means to have a deep, strong foundation. On 6 December 2013, Steve and Jacky Connelly went for a walk. They lived in Norfolk. The newspaper tells us that when they came back from their walk their house had been destroyed. Can you imagine that? It was the worst storm to hit Britain. Their house in Hemsby came off the cliff and on to the shore. O, how we need dig deep for our foundations in our life. We need deep and strong foundations.

Paul prays, that you might be 'rooted and established'. But what in? 'In love'! What did our Lord Jesus Christ say? 'By this everyone will know that you are my disciples, if you love one another' (John 13:35). Yes, be established in the love of God, but not just love *for* God, but the love *of* God to others also. And that you 'may have power with all the Lord's holy people, to grasp how wide and long and high and deep is the love of Christ and to know this love that surpasses knowledge' (Ephesians 3:18–19). I like that other word, 'grasp'. Paul is praying that you may grasp, that you may comprehend, that you may lay hold of how wide, how long, how high and how deep is the love of God.

> Could we with ink the oceans fill?
> And were the skies of parchment made,
> Were every stalk on earth a quill,
> And every man a scribe by trade;
> To write the love of God above
> Would drain the ocean dry,
> Nor could the scroll contain the whole,
> Though stretched from sky to sky.[4]

O, I want you to grasp the love of God in Christ. How wide and long and high and deep is that love! O believer you are loved, you are loved with a love that surpasses knowledge. 'O, the deep, deep, love of Jesus, vast, unmeasured, boundless, free!'[5] Or as Horatius Bonar's hymn says:

> O love of God, how strong and true!
> Eternal and yet ever new;
> Uncomprehended and unbought,
> Beyond all knowledge and all thought.[6]

And not just grasping but being filled, 'that you may be filled to the measure of all the fullness of God' (verse 19).

Honestly friends, we could spend months on this passage alone. What a statement! Paul is praying for the Ephesians, praying for Christians down the ages, that believers would be filled to the measure of all the fullness of God.

I don't know if you have been along to the youth work? The young people have been brilliant and they have been led brilliantly too, but they do put you through some difficult situations. I arrived there last night and there is a beach, and they wanted me to build two sandcastles. A beach! They have some water fights going on, they're supposed to be in Copacabana or wherever it was! O come with me this evening. We are going to leave Keswick. We are going on an aeroplane and we are going to go to somewhere like Hawaii. Are you with me? Palm trees, wonderful. And what's more, we are going to go to the edge of the shore and there's the Pacific Ocean, 63.8 million square miles, vast! It covers 46% of the earth's surface, it's 14,000 feet deep and stretches between Asia, Australia and America. And here, you and I are going to put our big toes in it. But because we are somewhere in Hawaii and the sun is burning down we decide to take a dip. We are going to dip into this vast, deep ocean. O, that you may be filled to the measure to all the fullness of God. O that we may dive into the ocean of his love. O that we might be filled!

My wife always tells me that I am boring when it comes to films. I like cowboy films and I like war films. I like the stories of the U-boats; how the U-boats used to go deep into the water, and how the depth that they went to was because of the water they allowed in. They allowed more and more water in so that they could go deeper and deeper and deeper and deeper. We need to know that power of his love and grace, by his Spirit, filling us, to the measure of the fullness of God. 'Father, establish your people.' Be established, rooted, grasping the length and breadth and height and depth of the love of God that surpasses knowledge and be filled to the measure of all the fullness of God.

Number three, be encouraged. Here is the apostle Paul chained to the Roman soldier. What would that Roman soldier think? Maybe he was converted by this prayer. But listen to how Paul ends this prayer, he ends with a doxology, verses 20–21:

> Now to him who is able to do immeasurably more than all we ask or imagine, according to his power that is at work within us, to him be glory in the church and in Christ Jesus throughout all generations for ever and ever! Amen.

'Now to him', actually we could have a whole sermon on just that phrase! To him! To him! The living God who, in the person of his Son, is altogether lovely, the fairest amongst ten thousand, the creator and sustainer of the universe – to him! 'To him who is able' – of course he is able! 'He is . . . able to save to the uttermost those that come to God through him' (Hebrews 7:25, NKJV). But he's not just able. This prayer gets higher and higher and higher and higher and higher, Paul is reaching a crescendo.

I know what some of you are thinking – 'O, he is just a scallywag from Liverpool.' You're right! Do you know that

Liverpool people like music? Have you heard of John, George, Paul and Ringo? They dominated the musical charts for years and years. Of course, when you are in such an august company as this you also need to remind folk of Sir Simon Rattle who at age thirteen conducted a philharmonic orchestra and has conducted wonderful orchestras around the world. And do you know, both the Beatles and Simon Rattle knew the power of moving on to crescendo? Now here's the apostle Paul, reaching a crescendo in prayer: 'Now to him who is able to do' – he is an active God, he is a living God! 'Immeasurably' – he is ageless and timeless and deathless and changeless and limitless. He is the infinite eternal one without limitation, without boundary, without measurement. He is able to do immeasurably more than all that we ask!

John Newton's hymn reminds us:

Thou art coming to a King:
Large petitions with thee bring;
For his grace and power are such,
None can ever ask too much.[7]

'Ask and it will be given to you; seek and you will find; knock and the door will be opened to you' (Matthew 7:7).

Be encouraged! He is able to do immeasurably more than all you ask! But it's not just that! He is able to do immeasurably more than we can think – he knows our thoughts, he knows our dreams. If this is limitless love and limitless power, 'to him be glory in the church and in Christ

Jesus throughout all generations for ever and ever! Amen' (verse 21).

I love the story of Philip Bliss. He was a poet and a teacher, a musician and an evangelist. He lived until he was thirty-eight years of age. In the very last year of his life, one of the very last things he did was go to a prison and preach the gospel. He was speaking to hard, tough prisoners. After some time he felt he was getting nowhere, so he began to sing a song he had written:

Man of sorrows! what a name
for the son of God, who came
ruined sinners to reclaim!
Hallelujah! what a Saviour!

The last verse says:

When he comes, our glorious King,
all his ransomed home to bring,
then anew his song we'll sing:
'Hallelujah! what a Saviour!'[8]

We will sing the song of the ages, hallelujah, 'to him be glory in the church and in Christ Jesus throughout all generations, for ever and ever! Amen' (verse 21).

How can you go on? Be empowered. Be established. Be encouraged.

Let us pray. 'Father, we are overwhelmed with the immensity of your grace and mercy towards us in Christ.

We are overwhelmed that unsearchable riches are credited to our account and that we are loved so much. Grant O Lord we pray, by your Spirit, that you will fill us anew. Empower us, establish us and encourage us as we continue through these shadowlands until we reach the glory land. For we ask this in the purest, wonderful and glorious name of Jesus.' Amen.

Notes

1. John Newton, 'Glorious things of thee are spoken', 1779.
2. Frederick W. Faber, 'My God, how wonderful thou art', 1849.
3. Kate Wilkinson, 'May the mind of Christ my Saviour', 1925.
4. Frederick Lehman, 'The love of God', 1917.
5. Samuel Francis, 'O the deep, deep love of Jesus', 1875.
6. Horatius Bonar, 'O love of God', 1861.
7. John Newton, 'Come my soul, thy suit prepare', 1779.
8. Philip Bliss, 'Man of sorrows', 1875.

week is over. Michael keeps nagging about singing to his sister, but kids are not allowed in ICU. Well, Karen works out that if he doesn't see his sister now, he may never see her alive. So she dresses him up in an oversized scrubs suit and marches him into ICU. He looks like a walking laundry basket. The head nurse recognizes him as a child and bellows, "Get that kid out of here now! No children allowed in ICU!" But the mother in Karen rises up strong, and this usually mild lady stared steely-eyed into the head nurse's face. Her lips are firm. "He is not leaving until he sings to his sister." Karen tows Michael to his sister's bedside. He gazes at the tiny infant losing the battle to live and he begins to sing. In the pure-hearted voice of a three-year-old he sings, "You are my sunshine." Instantly the baby girl responds. Her pulse rate becomes calm and steady. The ragged, strained breathing becomes as smooth as a kitten's purr. Michael's little sister relaxes as healing rest seems to sweep over her. The next day—the very next day—the little girl is well enough to go home. The medical staff just called it a miracle, but Karen called it a miracle of God's love.

Now, if God can take the song of a three-year-old to bring life physically to a dying child, can he not take the songs of his people when they worship him, to bring life to those who are not yet alive to him? Well, the apostle Paul says he can. Paul says when unbelievers come among you and hear the Words of God, "the secrets of their hearts are laid bare. So they will fall down and worship God, exclaiming, 'God is really among you!'" (1 Corinthians 14:24–25). That's what we long for in our churches isn't it?

The Bible Readings

Covenant Hits the Road

by Simon Manchester

Simon Manchester is the senior minister at St Thomas' Anglican Church, North Sydney. He is married to Kathy and they have three adult children. He was a school teacher before studying at Moore Theological College and he did training in Wollongong and London before taking up his first church in Sydney. He was chaplain for the North Sydney Rugby League Bears for seven seasons and also ran the ministry to the North Sydney business community for ten years.

Covenant Hits the Road: Deuteronomy 12 – 15

If you are a visitor today and you've not been here for the last two mornings, we are looking at the book of Deuteronomy, where Moses is preaching to God's people. They are on the edge of the Promised Land and he is preparing them to enter it. There is a structure to the thirty-four chapters of Deuteronomy. It begins with a little preamble, this is where we have been travelling. Then he focuses on the relationship we have with God who is with us, a relationship of privilege and responsibility. And then there is the unpacking of what this is going to look like and that's the section that we come to today and tomorrow, in chapters 12 – 26. The book ends with a section explaining: if you are not listening and obeying there will be trouble; if you are listening and are obeying there will be blessing; so a decision needs to be made.

So that is where the book goes and today we are up to this middle section.

Here Moses the preacher is unpacking the commandments, getting down to the specifics, and explaining what they look like in practice. I am persuaded that chapters 12 – 26 are an unpacking of the Ten Commandments. Chapter 12 is about worshipping God which sounds like commandment one. Chapter 13 is a warning on idolatry that sounds like commandment two. Deuteronomy 14 is about taking God's name for yourself and being a distinct people which sounds very much like commandment three. Deuteronomy 15 – 16 is about what to do in the seventh year and how to celebrate the feasts which sounds very much like the fourth commandment. And then you get to Deuteronomy 17 – 18 about authorities, which sounds very much like commandment five. Chapters 19 – 21 are about killing and war and sound like commandment six. Chapters 22 – 23 on marriage and relationships sound like commandment seven. Then in chapters 24 – 26 you get a whole lot of quick laws which have to do with speech and honesty which sound very much like commandments eight, nine, and ten. Not everybody thinks this, but I think there is a rough but real connection between the Ten Commandments, which we saw in chapter 5, and the unpacking that we are going to look at in chapters 12 – 26.

I want you to remember that Israel is a nation and therefore it has to pay taxes, but it is also a church and therefore it has to perform its ceremonies. So there are laws for civil behaviour and there are laws for church behaviour

– ceremonies. There are also laws to do with general morality. Now again, not everybody likes the idea of breaking the commandments up into moral, civil and ceremonial, but it's not a bad guide. And so, when non-Christians criticize you for sticking with heterosexual marriage but not sticking with food laws or penalties for stoning you just simply say, 'We are no longer a Middle East nation.' There is a big shift when you move from people in one land needing lots of laws for civil lifestyle, to the people of God living in various lands. And then of course there are the outward laws that we are reading in Deuteronomy which the Spirit of God internalizes and helps us live out.

We are going to look at this very practical section today and concentrate on how commands one to four are unpacked. We might call these the God-ward commands. Tomorrow we will look at some of the details of the man-ward commands, numbers five to ten. Remember that this teaching is the outworking of the covenant. Imagine you are talking to a newlywed couple and you ask, 'How does your marriage work?' And he says, 'Well I do the garbage on Thursday,' and she says, 'I do the ironing on Friday' or vice versa. You are waiting for them to say, 'We love each other, we live together and it's great.' The little job list is really a secondary thing. It's an outworking of a great relationship. And I hope that you know that all these details are the outworking of a great relationship with a covenant God. Chapters 12 – 26 are not a job interview to see whether you will get a job with God. You have a job with God and now he's going to talk to you like the staff, like his friends, like his family, about how the company works.

God is God – chapters 12 – 13

Look at Deuteronomy 12: 1–2: 'These are the decrees and laws you must be careful to follow in the land that the LORD, the God of your ancestors, has given you to possess – as long as you live in the land. Destroy completely all the places on the high mountains.' In other words, as God begins to unpack what the first commandment means, he tells his people, 'If you are going to worship me, you are going to have to destroy some rivals.' This is very blunt language – destroy, break down, smash, burn, cut down, wipe out, and get rid of everything which is a rival. So just as we expect someone who is engaged to break off their other relationships, or a recovering addict to put away temptations, we expect a serious Christian not to try to walk two paths at the same time, but walk one path with Jesus.

Now, when you think of the idols of Canaan, please don't be too dismissive. We think of those idols and wonder, 'How could you be so stupid?' But you know those idols were offering the people of Israel a huge amount of pleasure and security. In the same way, you might look at some of the idols I struggle with and think, 'That's so easy, just stop.' And I might look at some of the ones you wrestle with and think, 'Just don't do it.' But the idolatry that's in our hearts has been pushed at us by the world. The devil is roaming around like a roaring lion and therefore the principle of destroying, putting away, getting the axe out, is so important.

If you think this doesn't apply in the New Testament think of Colossians 3:5 where Paul says, 'Put to death . . .' You know when you're walking with Christ and something comes along and it's just your cup of idolatry and you say, 'Well I can indulge or I can just get the axe out.' The apostle says, 'Get the axe out!' And that will be for your joy and God's glory. We are not making this big sacrifice to earn Jesus, but in the light of the privilege of knowing Jesus we want to put away things that dishonour him and ruin us. That's what we think in our best moments isn't it? You remember that man in Matthew 13 who saw the treasure in the field and went and sold everything he had to get that field. I always imagine his family and friends saying, 'Have you seen the field? It's a mess, it's a swamp!' And he says, 'No, I've seen the treasure in the field, I'm getting rid of everything. It's all worth it.' And that's how we think in our best moments, we put away the stuff that wrecks and dishonours.

If you look at chapter 12:4 you'll see that God calls on Israel to worship him as he specifies: 'You must not worship the LORD your God in their way.' Verse 5, 'You are to seek the place'; verse 6, 'the sacrifices'; verse 7, 'the presence of God' with joy. Some theologians think that Moses is alluding to the eventual arrival in Jerusalem, but I think that's unlikely. I think Moses is simply saying, when it comes to worshipping God, he chooses the places you are to go to. This is an Old Testament position: go to the place, take the right sacrifice, do it in his presence and do it with joy.

Raymond Brown says in his Deuteronomy commentary that hundreds of new beliefs have come, even in the last twenty years, into this country.[1] They are basically bespoke religions. And can you guess the common ingredient of these new religions? They have no authority. So convenient! I do what I like. John Chapman used to say that if somebody presents you with a cup of black tea with four sugars and says, 'I brought this for you', there's tremendous sincerity there. But you actually like white coffee with no sugar. So although there has been some sincerity, it's wrong, it's not what's being asked for. It's not a bad thing to ask, 'What would you like if I go and get you a drink?' And it's not a bad thing to say to the Lord, 'What are you asking me for?' And the answer comes back here in Deuteronomy 12: 'I want you to worship before me, where I say, how I say, and with great joy.'

So God's people are not to invent gods but they are called to respond to him as he specifies. We know that when we are walking with the Lord there is great freedom. Freedom is not me taking my tiny little self and naively going off into the unknown and doing what I want, it's finding the place where God says I will meet him. And of course to be in God's fellowship is to come to Jesus. And to walk in God's fellowship is to walk with Jesus. Now we know when God talks about worship he means much more than singing. I hope, friends, that you won't let yourself or others strangle worship and turn it into the few minutes of singing at 11 o'clock on a Sunday. Remember that worship is where your body goes, Romans 12. Therefore as you walk you worship, as you drive home you worship, as you go shopping you worship and as you go back behind the front door you worship. Your life is worship to a worthy God.

And when we do treat God as God, look at the effects, look at chapter 12:15 where he says, 'Eat as much of the meat as you want.' 'Don't eat the blood,' he says, 'but do eat in my presence, walk in fellowship with me and enjoy yourself.' Enjoy yourself! There are shades of Genesis 1 and 2 here. God's fellowship is like that tremendous paradise. Remember Jesus said he'd come to bring life and life to the full. How many of us grow up thinking that Jesus destroys and the devil gives life, only later to discover that the devil destroys and Jesus gives life to the full?

We come to chapter 13, one of the most shocking chapters in the Bible. The chapter basically says that when you come across idolatry destroy it. And as we read this chapter we are meant to shake in our boots as I think that the Israelites were meant to shake in their boots. But like a surgeon removing a cancer, like a policeman removing a bomb, like a father removing an intruder, God calls on his people Israel to remove idolatry because idolatry spells death and God takes death seriously. And if a smaller death will prevent a bigger death, then says the Lord, 'Go and do it.'

In Deuteronomy 13:1–5 we meet the idolatrous prophet. These people of course are always dangerous because they have got the ability to persuade with success, just like a spellbinding preacher. But there is all the difference in the world between somebody who is spellbindingly capable and likely to persuade the gullible and the true prophet who is actually speaking the words of God. You need to be extremely careful.

Now friends we mustn't wait for non-Christians to appreciate Deuteronomy 13. Non-Christians would not see that idolatry is a cancer, a bomb, an intruder. They can only see temporal dangers, but you can see spiritual dangers and the New Testament tells us that we are to take action when idolatry is being preached or promoted.

The second group in chapter 13 is the family idolater and this is even more serious (verses 6–11). This is such a difficult section to read because here is somebody coming to tempt you with idolatry and it is your daughter, your wife, your closest friend. This section is meant to rattle the cage of everybody who reads it. I don't know of anyone in the Old Testament who actually went and killed false prophets, except Elijah. But here was the warning and no doubt the deterrent that these false prophets were to be killed in order that Israel will be afraid. So can you see the point? A very clever, dynamic and successful person comes and says, 'Let's worship other gods' and the Lord says, 'It's time to stone him.' That's the Old Testament. In the New Testament it's time to silence him – take away his ministry or walk away from it.

And the third group in chapter 13 is where there is a whole town given to idolatry and in danger of infecting that nation. If you look at verse 14 it says, 'you must enquire, probe and investigate' – in other words don't do anything too quickly, make a serious investigation. Then, there is to be complete action – destroy the town. And again I don't know of any examples of this but it's a reminder that for the Lord idolatry is so dreadful and for the people of God so deadly.

When you get to the New Testament, idolatry is still deadly but it's not the same judgment that God is accelerating here in the Old Testament. So we might command a false teacher to be quiet or we might remove the immoral, unrepentant person who is bringing the fellowship into disrepute. But basically we should be putting our sins to death which wreck our fellowship with God. We are so thankful for our Saviour, because we are idolaters and without him we would have no hope. Peter tells us the perfect Saviour died for the idolater, to bring you to God; and that's our security, our joy and our thanksgiving.

Death and Life

Chapter 14 is a fascinating chapter dealing with shaving, food and tithing. You begin to realize that God is interested in everything. He's interested in death and life. He's interested in reaching into the very kitchen of your home and the very pockets of your trousers. When he says don't cut or shave for the dead he simply means don't react to death like a pagan. Because pagans do things that indicate they are distraught or distressed without hope, and you are not to respond like that. Think of what Paul says in 1 Thessalonians 4: don't grieve without hope, grieve with hope.

The Old Testament of course was very shadowy on the afterlife but there was still great hope. We know that in Psalm 23 David talks about being in his Father's house for ever and Psalm 16 speaks of treasures at God's right hand. Job declared:

> I know that my redeemer lives,
> and that in the end he will stand on the earth.
> And after my skin has been destroyed,
> yet in my flesh I will see God.
> (Job 19:25–26)

We see hints of the afterlife in Isaiah 25 – 26, 35, and Daniel 12. It's shadowy, but it's there. And therefore God's people were not to respond to death as if it was the end. They weren't to be pessimistic, cutting themselves and shaving themselves. They weren't to be optimistic, as if nothing matters. But they were to be realistic, they were to feel the loss and also hold the hope. Some of you who have lost loved ones will know how important it is to feel the grief and hold the hope.

Funerals in my country, and perhaps here, are becoming either silly celebrations with balloons as if nothing has happened or they are utterly filled with sadness and tragic grief. And, the Christian is able, by the grace of God, to walk through this, feeling the loss, holding the hope. We are not in fairy land, this is a reality, Christ has risen and he's given us hope. We are able to look back into someone's life with gratitude, we are able to look forward with certainty in a way only a Christian can. Back and forward, back over eighty years and forward into a billion years and beyond.

And then in chapter 14:3–21 we get the famous food laws. What do you make of them? First of all this is not a hygiene issue. It's not even, 'this is what pagans eat, so you must eat something different'. This is a list where, simply and basically, God decides. In the sovereignty of God he says, 'I am choosing the clean and I am choosing the unclean.' And friends do you see the genius of this? Every time you went shopping you would remember that there was a clean, elect people of God living among an unclean set of nations needing to know the Lord. Every time you sat at breakfast, lunch and dinner you would say to yourself, 'We are so blessed to be God's clean people. Not because we are clean ourselves, but because he has chosen and made us clean.' So every shopping visit was a lesson, every meal was a lesson: God has chosen us and we are seeking to live for him.

Now these food laws of course were abolished in the New Testament. Jesus declared food to be clean (Matthew 7) and he taught Peter to eat freely in Acts 10 and 11. Why did he do this? Because the Jew–Gentile distinctions have gone in Jesus. Everyone who comes to Jesus is in that privileged position. Jesus kept the law in order to save us from the law and when we belong to him he removes all the barriers and he, the clean dying for the unclean, makes us his clean people.

The last section of chapter 14 is where we are told that Israel was to have new values. They were to tithe or to give a tenth of their produce, and eat it in God's presence. When you get to the New Testament the tithe is gone. The closest you get to a tithe in the New Testament is 1 Corinthians where Paul says to set aside a portion of your giving for the Lord's work.

I remember hearing of a lady who came up to her pastor and gave him fifty dollars for the building project. He said, 'That's wonderful. I'll accept it if it is a true representation of how the Lord has blessed you.' She quite ashamedly took it back and she came up to him the next Sunday and said, 'Here's five thousand dollars for the Lord's project.' And he said, 'That's wonderful. I'll accept it if it's a true reflection of how the Lord has blessed you.' And the next week she came up with fifty thousand dollars and she said, 'This is a reflection of how the Lord has blessed me.' We are to give by grace. We are not hemmed in by law. We have the privilege, the opportunity, to give in a way that reflects how God has blessed us. So do you see what chapter 14 is all about? It begins by saying life and death is completely different for the believer, your daily life is completely different for the believer and it goes right to the very wallets and purses of your lives because God has been so gracious to you.

Freedom and Joy

Now we are going to look at Deuteronomy 15 and 16 which relates to the fourth commandment about the

Sabbath. And it is interesting that there is so much joy for God's people. There are really no oppressive rules. God says in chapter 15:1 that every seven years debts were to be cancelled. Well, what a lovely group to be a part of. There you are, you have money owing to somebody and up comes the seventh year and all debts are cancelled. Suddenly there is a great hope for the poor people and freedom for the rich. The nations are looking on and seeing the people of God surviving and being looked after and they say, 'What God is this?' What a witness to the church, what a witness to the world! Now friends the New Testament doesn't legislate on this, but the principles are clear aren't they? We are meant to provide as best as we can for the fellowship. 2 Corinthians 8 – 9 demonstrates wonderful fellowship when the apostle Paul says to the churches in Greece, 'Would you join together to help me look after the poor in Jerusalem? What a witness this will be!'

Can I also say as a slight aside, don't try to solve global poverty. The world is gospel poor and the great riches that we have to give to the world is the gospel, anything else is a bonus. But we want to make sure that the gospel is driving what we are doing. We mustn't try and take on the whole world as if suddenly this minority could solve the majority poverty.

In Deuteronomy 16 God says celebrate the feasts. He mentions Passover, when you remember your rescue; Pentecost, where you remember the start of the harvest; and Tabernacles, where you are in your little tents and booths and you remember how God wonderfully sustains you through the wilderness. And he says twice, verses 11 and 14, 'be joyful' because you are focusing on your rescue, on your salvation and you belong to the Lord from your start until your finish. 'He who began a good work in you will carry it on to completion until the day of Christ Jesus (Philippians 1:6).

So this is how God instructed Israel. But we read in Psalm 106 they did not destroy what the Lord commanded, they mingled with the nations, adopted their customs, worshipped their idols and fell into their snares. Because the law doesn't change the heart. That's why our world is struggling to control itself with legislation.

I remember listening to Charles Colson when he came to Sydney. He said, 'Every morning I would walk into the Oval Office and there would be Henry Kissinger, Richard Nixon, myself and maybe one or two others. Henry Kissinger would come in with a big bundle of folders and drop them down on his desk and he said, "Mr President, today we are going to change world history."' And Colson said, 'We just shuffled the papers. We just moved them around the desk; we didn't change anything because until the heart is changed nothing really changes.'

That's why today we are so thankful for the Lord Jesus, the one who can change the heart. We put our faith in him who died for us and he puts his life in us. We are not perfect. We are forgiven, we are in his family, we have a future and he helps us day-by-day to live for him. This is the message of Deuteronomy: preaching the Word of God, pre-framed by the Israel of God, practised by the Son of God, producing a new people of God.

Note

1. Raymond Brown, *The Message of Deuteronomy* (IVP, 1993).

God's Kingdom – Glorious and Without End

by Steve Brady

Steve Brady was born in Liverpool where he was converted in his teens. He is married to Brenda and has two children and four grandchildren. After a number of pastorates, he is presently Principal of Moorlands College, a trustee of Keswick Ministries, and author of a number of books including *Colossians* and *Galatians* in the Keswick Study Guide series, and *The Incredible Journey*, an Advent book published by BRF. A keen sportsman, he hates gardening and still has an irrational attachment to Everton Football Club!

God's Kingdom – Glorious and Without End: Revelation 20 – 22

Some of you know that I used to be a pastor in the East End of London and when our kids were nine and just coming up six, we were called down to sunny Bournemouth. It wasn't until we got there that we realized my son was struggling with maths. But help was at hand. A lady in the church said, 'I can help him get up to speed. I'm a maths tutor.' So every week he would go for some extra tuition – you can imagine how happy he was about this arrangement! And then, after a little while, he seemed to take off like a Harrier Jump Jet. She came to me and said, 'Your Paul's doing well at maths,' and I said, 'Yes!' She said, 'Do you know why?' And I said, 'It must be your excellent tuition.' 'No, no,' she said, 'I don't know if you've noticed but the answers are all in the back of the workbook. He's just been copying them in. He got one out of kilter and kept going so they are all right if you move them down one.' His sins had found him out!

What do you do when your kid does that? I thought, 'I'll take him out for a celebratory ice cream because my kid's a smart kid!' He'd learnt a big lesson that too many Christians haven't. He didn't care what the maths might be – whether it was multiplication, division, algebra – because he knew that if he turned to the back of the book he'd always get the right answer!

And whatever we make of this amazing book of Revelation the big, big story is the Lord Jesus is on the throne of the universe and 'the kingdom of this world has become the kingdom of our Lord and of his Messiah and he will reign for ever and ever' (Revelation 11:15). If we fail to see the Lord, we've really missed the central point of this amazing book. As we turn to these final chapters, there are three aspects of God's kingdom – his rule and reign in Christ – I want us to note: its millennial, eternal, and here-and-now phases.

1. The Millennial Kingdom – Chapter 20

Here we may note three large issues for our attention, expressed as: four facts that are demonstrable, five areas that are debatable, and one truth that is declarable.

Firstly, four facts that are *demonstrable*: verses 1–3, the binding of Satan; verses 4–6, the reign of the saints; verses 7–10, the loosing of Satan for a season; and verses 11–15, the judgment of the world.

Secondly, five areas that are *debatable*. Question one: who are the souls, verse 5? Are they all the Christian dead at the end of time? Or are they those who have undergone a spiritual rebirth, here called 'the first resurrection' (verse 5), that brings them to spiritual life? As our Lord says in John 5:25, there is a spiritual coming to life now for those who hear 'the voice of the Son of God'. In that same gospel passage, such a 'first resurrection' is followed by the final, general resurrection of all 'in their graves' (John 5:28); hence, two resurrections are indicated, spiritual and physical. Is that the point here in Revelation 20?

The second question is, where do they reign? Well that's obvious, it's on earth, isn't it? But we may notice that they are described as 'on thrones', so may that then locate them in heaven? In other words, do the Christian dead reign now?

Hard on the heels of that question, our third asks, when does Satan's binding take place? Some say we must await the millennium because clearly Satan has free rein in the world now. Right? Really! How easy to forget the cross, that decisive moment in space–time history upon which the whole future of the universe turns. When Christ died for our sins he disarmed the principalities and powers (see Colossians 2:14–15). So how is the world being 'undeceived'? Through the preaching of the gospel and the reign of Christ in believers' hearts and lives!

Fourthly, the question arises as to whether there will be an ultimate spiritual showdown, the final battle? Of course, there is a spiritual battle going on all the time: the devil never takes vacations! But that does not preclude a final battle because, as I've mentioned in the previous studies, Revelation can be viewed like a snowball rolling down a hill. The snowball may be travelling in one direction, but it is also gathering mass and intensity. Likewise, I believe there will be a final showdown before the coming of the Lord.

And fifthly, what about the thousand years? Is it literal or symbolical? The answer to that will depend on whether you are pre-, post-, a-, or just-confused millennialist!

But there is one truth that is totally *declarable*. In the interim, things may get worse but they will get wonderfully, eternally better! How much worse? The devil, as chapter 12 records, has been thrown down to earth, and is 'filled with fury because he knows his time is short' (12:12). However, here we are reminded of the certainty of judgment, and evil's demise (20:10–15). And how much better? Welcome to the Kingdom's glorious phase.

2. The Eternal Kingdom – Chapters 21 and 22

Do you recall the BBC programme, *Tomorrow's World*? Well, here it is in reality and fullness – *a new heaven and a new earth*. This is the goal of the whole great storyline of the Bible – Eden lost, Eden restored, Eden plus, plus, plus, and on and on, into eternity, wonderfully for ever! In our world today, there is what has been termed 'a universal homesickness'. C. S. Lewis captured the idea beautifully when he wrote about only 'the scent of a flower we have not found, the echo of a tune we have not heard, news from a country we have never yet visited'.[1]

There is a sense of paradise lost in the human heart. A restlessness, a longing, a hope that one day there may be a better world. Sometimes, it is foreshadowed in peace movements, or a desire for a pristine world where we get rid of all the tat and ecological chaos we cause. But what is it we are waiting for? What is heaven?

A man bumped into an old school friend who was a Christian. He asked after the welfare of the Christian's wife, whom he had heard was ill. 'Oh, she's in heaven,' came the reply. His friend responded, 'Oh, I am sorry to hear that,' which did not sound right. 'I mean, I'm really glad to hear that' – that didn't sound any better. Finally, he hit on, 'Well, I am surprised!' Hmm!

'Heaven' is a tricky word to define, even in the Bible. Sometimes it means God himself, in his infinite being and his eternal location: 'I've sinned,' said the prodigal, 'against heaven' (Luke 15:18, 21). Sometimes, the sky is meant, or the heavens which declare God's glory (Psalm 19:1, Revelation 6:13). Other times, believers talk about heaven being in their heart. There's a truth in that because when we become Christians God puts a little bit of heaven, the first fruits of his Spirit as it is called, into our heart, to prepare us for the glory to come. We now have a spiritual homing device within.

Again, there is an intermediate heaven. Am I going to heaven when I die? I believe I am, and my next conscious moment will be, 'away from the body and at home with the Lord' (2 Corinthians 5:8). Some will remember we spent a little time on Revelation 6: 9–11, looking at the state of righteous dead. They worship, wait, wonder, and are there through no merit of their own, but because they are washed in the blood of Christ (Revelation 7:13).

Finally, there is an inherited heaven, the ultimate state, the new heaven and the new earth. The resurrection of believers is the stark reminder that the future state is an embodied one in a whole new space, additionally called 'the Holy City' (21:2). So, although we will be changed into the likeness of Christ (1 John 3:1–2), there will still be continuity. You will be truly yourself and so will I! Intriguingly, we are told there is 'no longer any sea' (21:1). Why? I take this to be a metaphor, one that runs throughout Scripture. The sea, especially in the Old Testament, is often a picture of chaos; that which is out of kilter; of brokenness and separation from God. In that final state, however, all the storms of life are over, no more painful separations from the Lord and others are experienced, and all life's dark and perplexing secrets are resolved.

As the narrative unfolds, the Holy City is portrayed as a place and people, God's people. And it is a reality that humankind has not built, since this city comes down from God (21:2). Here is the death knell for all human utopias, whether they be the ancient Roman Empire, Marxist regimes or so-called Islamic State. This is God's city, his work. A city, however, needs a number of things to function, like basic *security*, an issue large on the agenda of every government. Here in the UK, we now have terrorism prevention policies appearing everywhere in order to suppress violent extremism. God's city is secure – just check out the wonderfully thick walls – no security problems here (21:17–18).

When we lived in east London, we had a number of break-ins. The most memorable was the first, when a thief came in during the night. They took a pint of milk, a pound of cheese out of the fridge, a cassette player, a radio and a whole pile of what they thought were music cassettes. One of them was my preaching on 'Thou shalt not steal'! I hoped they'd bring back all the knocked-off gear when they listened to the cassette – they didn't!

There is also *community* here, illustrated in a number of ways. 'I heard a loud voice from the throne saying, "Look! God's dwelling place is now among the people, and he will dwell with them"' (21:3). Or again, the names of the twelve tribes of Israel are written on the gates, and the names of the twelve apostles written on the foundations (21:12–14). At the end of time, there is one great, united family of God. The barrier, the dividing wall of hostility between Jew and non-Jew, broken down in Christ (Ephesians 2:14), has produced the one people of the Lord, sharing eternity. 'In Christ', we see that it doesn't really matter where we have come from, it only matters to whom we belong and where we are going.

And there's heaven's *immensity*. Note the measurements – 12,000 stadia cubed (21:16) – 1,400 miles × 1,400 miles × 1,400 miles. So how many cubic miles is that? I'll tell you – a lot! It's huge, massive. Why? Because there is room here for everyone who comes to Christ. Sharing the gospel personally and through your church is not some sideshow in history, some religious eccentricity. It is the master-plan and the Master's plan of the ages to bring countless sinners home as sons and daughters of God – 'a great multitude that no one could count' (Revelation 7:9).

This city is marked by *purity*, since 'nothing impure will ever enter it' (21: 27). That's why the note of judgment at the end of chapter 20 is so important, and none should speak about judgment lightly, without tears in our eyes and heaviness on our hearts. There is a heaven to gain and a hell to shun, that makes human decisions really important, and gospel witness essential and urgent. Some folks say, 'Well, I don't get it. Why can't God just change everybody?' Because part of our humanity is having this wonderful and wretched thing called 'free will'. We are not automatons, pre-programmed always to obey. We make our own choices. Have you ever thought what it would be like if heaven were stuffed with people who didn't want to be there, who hated God and his worship and praise? To them, it would feel like hell. That's why it always surprises me when people think 'church', or more precisely being with believers, is something they'd like to opt out of, preferring their leisure and pleasures, and yet want to go to heaven one day! Really? You can't stand an hour in God's presence with his people once a week, yet hope to spend eternity with them where the praise is 24/7? That's why we need to be 'born again', to have a little bit of heaven in our hearts now to prepare us for then.

And do note the wonderful brightness, the *luminosity* of this city, verses 23–25:

> The city does not need the sun or the moon to shine on it, for the glory of God gives it light, and the Lamb is its lamp. The nations will walk by its light, and the kings of the earth will bring their splendour into it. On no day will its gates ever be shut, for there will be no night there.

These biblical metaphors of light and darkness are actually universal metaphors. O. Henry, the American writer, repines, 'Turn up the lights, I don't want to go home in the dark.'[2] When we belong to Christ, we never do. Heaven is a place where there is no more darkness. Some of us know how hard nights are. But Jesus is the light of that heavenly city. Hallelujah!

And what will we do? Will it be boring? Some people imagine we'll be seated on a cloud of cotton wool, strumming a harp for ever and ever. That's why a lot of folk are not in a hurry to go to heaven. They fear it will be like singing *Songs of Fellowship* book 799 zillion for the zillionth time! That's because, at that point, we have lost sight of the Lord! So these images here are meant to fire our imaginations and fill our hearts and minds with joy and expectancy. So, heaven is a place of incredible *vitality*.

Of course, there are lots we do not and cannot know yet. That said, the truth is we all have questions we'd at least some kind of answer for. So, for example, will we have *memory* there? Well, as our memory is tied in with our identity, of being you, there are things we will of course remember. Otherwise, imagine chatting to someone for a millennium or more, then discovering you did have a lot in common – you were married to that person for fifty-three years! So, naturally, we will know each other. But, I believe, it will be a redeemed memory. The dark things, I think, we will not remember. And the bright things? Ah! Yes! I'll never forget 9.15 p.m. on 13 March 1967, when 'I came to Jesus as I was, weary and worn and sad; I found in him a resting-place and he has made me glad.'[3] You'll also have abundant memories of the Lord's grace to you.

Will there be *time*? Let's try an experiment. If you are able, please raise your arms? (Quick a photograph! Keswick's gone totally charismatic!) Now put them down again. So, we can raise our arms and put them down again – that's a sequence. Will you be able to do that with your resurrection body? Oh, yes! And that's a form of time. Some people think the eternal state is a timeless eternity. No, that's not what the Bible teaches! There will be a time there, but without its tyranny. C. S. Lewis spoke of it as like our time only thicker.[4] Of course, there will be time otherwise you couldn't have music could you? It would just be a noise. One poet, Steve Turner, suggests that whoever else in heaven is not needed – musicians certainly are! We will worship God like we've never worshipped before. If you really want to know what biblical worship is like, just go through these great doxologies in Revelation for a start! They are focused on all that God is and has done for us in

Christ. Christian worship is God-centred, Christ-focused, and Spirit-inspired.

Will there be *growth*? I love that Ephesians talks about the 'unsearchable riches of Christ' (3:8). The word has the implication of being un-mappable, unfathomable, we'll-never-come-to-the-endable of. We'll need all eternity, as finite, resurrected, glorified beings to get to just the outer edges of the riches of the infinite, wonderful, triune God, whom we love and worship.

What about *animals*? Will there be animals in that final state? What about Isaiah 11:6 and the wolf lying down with the lamb, for example? Some say, 'Well that's just the millennium.' It might be, but I think the indications are that all created life is somehow represented in the new heaven and new earth. Now please don't leave Keswick saying, 'Steve Brady thinks there is hope for my little Toby, my little pet poodle!' I haven't said that, because I haven't met your little Toby! But the truth is, we must not think of that eternal state as boring. Will we have cars? I think we will, because of that song, 'what wonder, what *transport* when Jesus we see'![5] (OK, I am joking!)

Finally, we head to a new depth of *intimacy* in that eternal home. This is portrayed in a number of ways: 'he will dwell with them' (21:3); there is no temple (21:22) because God is everywhere; this city is a perfect cube (21:16). Why? Because that is precisely what the ancient Holy of Holies in Solomon's temple was (1 Kings 6:20). Now, this whole city, this whole new creation, is a holy of holies. And, wonderfully, we will see the Lord: 'they will see his face and his name will be on their foreheads' (22:4). This is termed the beatific vision. That's what we are made for. The most dreadful thing about our humanity and sinfulness is, 'though the eye of sinful man, thy glory may not see.'[6] Sin blinds us to this glorious, amazing God, so no one can look on him and live. But now grace has prepared us for the vision of God, the thought captured so beautifully in some of our older hymns: 'the sons of ignorance and night' are dwelling 'in the eternal light through the eternal love'; and again, 'And I shall see him face to face and tell the story, saved by grace.'[7]

3. The Here-and-Now Kingdom – Chapter 22:6–21

Is this all 'pie in the sky when you die' stuff? Is it believable? How in the here-and-now can faith be sustained? Well, it really comes down to whom we trust. Powerfully, we are reminded that the one who speaks to us is the Lord himself: 'He who was seated on the throne said, "I am making everything new!" Then he said, "Write this down, for these words are trustworthy and true"' (Revelation 21:5). Likewise, the same emphasis emerges in the next chapter: 'These words are trustworthy and true' (22:6). In whom do we trust? To put it practically, it means to trust our Bibles, to trust what God has told us in this book. In the words of 2 Peter, 'We did not follow cleverly devised stories when we told you about the coming of our Lord Jesus Christ in power, but we were eye-witnesses of his majesty' (1:16); that's why we need to be Bible-centred. This book, divided into 1,189 chapters, 929 in the Old Testament, 260 in the New, is the Word of our God. And when every other agony aunt and uncle is pensioned off, and every other prognosticator and cynic is forgotten, 'the Word of our God stands for ever' (Isaiah 40:8). That being the case, fittingly we are reminded not to add or take away from these Words of our God (Revelation 22:18–19).

And in the here and now, three times we are reminded, by the Lord Jesus himself: 'I am coming soon' (22:7, 12, 20). 'Well, Lord, you seem to have delayed so long. Have we missed something?' Does 'soon' mean 'immediately'? No, it means 'imminently', perhaps 'surprisingly' might capture the idea. Why? So that every day, we might anticipate and look forward to his coming, and therefore live each day to his glory. More of that as I conclude.

Because the Lord is returning, what kind of churches do we need? In a phrase, we need responsive and obedient ones. 'Look, I am coming soon! Blessed is the one who keeps the words of the prophecy written in this book' (22:7). So, we need to walk closely with Christ, worship our God (22:8, 9), staying spiritually clean: 'Blessed are those who wash their robes, that they may have the right to the tree of life and may go through the gates into the city' (22:14). We need to keep short accounts with God and others, if we can, not only between Keswicks, but every day. Let's daily and hourly respond to the invitation: 'The Spirit and the bride say, "Come!" And let the one who hears say, "Come!" Let the one who is thirsty come; and let the one who wishes take the free gift of the water of life' (22:17).

> I heard the voice of Jesus say,
> 'Behold, I freely give
> the living water, thirsty one;
> stoop down and drink and live.'
> I came to Jesus, and I drank
> of that life-giving stream;
> my thirst was quenched, my soul revived,
> and now I live in him.[8]

As we close, may I ask a number of questions? First, and most importantly, are you going to heaven? Have you trusted Christ, have you abandoned yourself to him? We need the Lord Jesus Christ now in life to prepare us for death and the life beyond. Think of it this way: life is like a road's box junction. The Highway Code tells us not to enter the box junction until your exit is clear. Oh, please, I beg of you, don't enter the box junction of death without Christ. He is the Lord of the living and the dead, for he has risen from the dead. Why would you want to leave this life without him, and enter eternity to face him not as Saviour but as Judge? What folly! Trust him while you may, walk with him, and he will never leave or forsake you in life or death, and will love you for ever.

My second question is, are you seeking to take others with you? Are you reminding others that there is an ultimate, wonderful and eternal home – the kingdom of God – and it will all be worth it in the end? To quote a John Newton hymn:

> Saviour, if of Zion's city
> I through grace a member am,
> Let the world deride or pity,
> I will glory in thy name.
> Fading is the worldling's pleasure,
> All his boasted pomp and show;
> Solid joys and lasting treasures
> None but Zion's children know.[9]

Or, as C. S. Lewis put it at the end of his seven-volume *Narnia Chronicles*:

> All their life in this world and all their adventures of Narnia had only been the cover and title page: now at last they were beginning Chapter One of the Great Story which no one on earth has read: which goes on for ever: in which every chapter is better than the one before.[10]

Wow! Hallelujah!

Notes

1. C. S. Lewis, *The Weight of Glory* (William Collins, 2013).
2. C. Alphonso Smith, *O. Henry Biography 1916* (Cornell University Library, 2009).
3. Horatius Bonar, 'I heard the voice of Jesus say', 1846.
4. C. S. Lewis, *Letters to Malcolm* (Mariner Books, 2007).
5. Fanny Crosby, 'To God be the glory', 1875.
6. Reginald Heber, 'Holy, holy, holy', 1861.

7. Thomas Binney, 'Eternal light', 1826; Fanny Crosby, 'Saved by grace', 1891.
8. Horatius Bonar, ibid.
9. John Newton, 'Glorious things of thee are spoken', 1779.
10. C. S. Lewis, *The Last Battle* (HarperCollins, 2001).

The Sacrificial Servant

by David Jackman

After graduation and some years in teaching, David worked with UCCF among university students, before theological studies and then serving for fifteen years on the staff of Above Bar Church, Southampton. In 1991, he moved to London as the founder-director of the Cornhill Training Course, a ministry of the Proclamation Trust, which seeks to train and develop a new generation of biblical preachers. Latterly, he served as its President. He is married to Heather and they have two married children and four grand-children. Based in London in retirement, he is actively involved in a ministry of writing, expository preaching and biblical training at home and overseas.

The Sacrificial Servant: Isaiah 53

Well, this morning we are treading on holy ground. If the book of Isaiah is one of the mountain ranges of the Old Testament, clearly chapter 53 is one of its most majestic peaks. There is a danger that it is familiar ground to us and I am praying that God will help us see new things, as well as revisit old and much-loved truths, as we focus on the sacrificial servant.

The servant is the major focus of Isaiah 40 – 55. His person and work are primarily revealed in a series of four poems which are often called the 'servant songs'. Now we could have a whole series of Bible studies on these, each of them sets out the character and work of the servant and is followed by God's explanation of the implications of that work. We are onlookers, we are being instructed and inspired by these songs.

Our passage is a beautifully crafted poem with five stanzas or sections of gradually increasing length. Each stanza represents three verses in our version of Isaiah's text. And what is fascinating is that the first and the last sections balance each other by repeating the same theme which is the servant's great victory and triumph. Stanzas two and four also balance one another as they explore the facts about the servant's humiliation; his death and burial. And then right in the middle, verses 4–6, the third stanza, is the heart of the poem where the meaning is fully explained. The heart of the matter is that this servant is producing a salvation which depends upon his own self-sacrificing love. So here we have a very carefully crafted poem in which the central concept is the sacrificial death of the servant. If verses 4–6 are the middle, then the middle of the middle is verse 5 and this is the central message of this passage:

> But he was pierced for our transgressions,
>   he was crushed for our iniquities;
> the punishment that brought us peace was on him,
>   and by his wounds we are healed.

Now, my friends, this means that the heart of evangelical gospel theology is the cross of our Lord Jesus Christ. Of course, the incarnation is vitally important; he is *Immanuel*, God with us. It affirms that Jesus is both truly God and truly man and that is essential as it is only by the death of the Son of God that that great work of atonement in time and for eternity could be accomplished. Our sin could only be dealt with, the holiness of God could only be propitiated, when the Son of God came and bore our sins in his body on the cross. So right at the heart of our theology there lies this conviction that the Lord Jesus is dying in our place, bearing the penalty for our sin. And Jesus himself clearly embraced this, he took upon himself the role of the servant. In Luke 22:37 Jesus applied Isaiah 53 to himself: 'It is written: "And he was numbered with the transgressors"; and I tell you that this must be fulfilled in me. Yes, what is written about me is reaching its fulfilment.' So Jesus says, 'Isaiah 53 is about me.' And I want to look at this chapter and seek to meet the Lord Jesus, our Saviour, in these five stanzas of this amazing song.

I want to do it by asking a question, which I think each stanza answers. So here is my first question: Who can this servant be? (Isaiah 52:13–15). If you look at the immediate context there is a call to leave Babylon (Isaiah 52:11). A new exodus is happening, the exile is ending. The song explains how it is going to be achieved. Look at those first three verses, they present us with contrasts which are mind boggling. So in verse 13 the servant is 'high', 'lifted up' and 'exalted'. If you want to put it in New Testament terms, he is risen, ascended and glorified. This will be the result, we are told, of the servant acting wisely. The verb here means 'knowing what to do to achieve a result.' Some translations talk about 'success' here. He does the right thing in order that the purpose may be fulfilled.

But it is not just that. Look at verse 14 – his appearance is marred, he is disfigured, he is an appalling sight! So on the one hand you have a risen, ascended, glorified one – and all these are metaphors of kingship – and then, on the other hand, you have this beaten, broken, bruised man who hardly seems to be like a human being, he has been so abused and maltreated.

So what is the mystery here? Who can this be? Well, read on to verse 15:

> So he will sprinkle many nations,
> and kings will shut their mouths because of him.
> For what they were not told, they will see,
> and what they have not heard, they will understand.

This mysterious servant is going to have widespread and profound effects on the nations, on the kings, the rulers of the world. They are going to be dumbfounded as their eyes are opened and their understanding is instructed by what this servant is going to accomplish. Well, this marks him out as unique in the history of the world. But the key to the mystery is there at the start of verse 15, 'he will sprinkle many nations'. That is an Old Testament technical term for performing a purification rite, sprinkling the altar with the blood of sacrifice. So the servant's suffering brings purification and cleansing to the nations, who, under Old Testament law, are excluded from the covenants of promise. Through the servant's work the nations will be brought into a covenant relationship with God. It was a revolutionary idea in the Old Testament. So who can this servant be? We are in the privileged position of knowing the answer to that question. We can say, 'This is the Son of God, who loved me and gave himself for me.'

The Lord Jesus – buffeted, beaten, scourged and whipped to within an inch of his life; his face lacerated by the crown of thorns; almost unrecognizable as a human being – that is how God sprinkles the nations. And that is how a holy God can accept you and me into his presence. When Charles Spurgeon, the great nineteenth-century preacher, was asked to sum up the gospel in a sentence, he famously said, 'It is four words – Jesus died for me.'[1] Those four words resonate with meaning don't they? Jesus, and all that he stands for, died as the sacrificial atonement for me.

> Bearing shame and scoffing rude,
> In my place condemned he stood,
> Sealed my pardon with his blood;
> Hallelujah! what a Saviour![2]

Our second question, verses 1–3, what is he like? What's the description of this servant? And verse 1 picks up the idea from Isaiah 52:15 of this strong note of incredulity. 'Who has believed our message and to whom has the arm of the Lord been revealed?' To paraphrase this you could say, 'Whoever could have imagined that the arm of the Lord would be revealed this way? Can this really be the arm of the Lord?' You know when we get the 'Lord' in capital letters there in our English translations, it takes us back to the Hebrew word *Yahweh* or *Jehovah*. It's the name he gave to Moses, 'I am who I am, the God who never changes, the God who is always faithful to his promises, the God of covenant mercy who continually cares for his people.' Is this Lord, the Lord of the mighty arm, the Lord of great deliverance, really going to act this way? Surely if God is going to intervene in the world he will do it in a display of great power, magnificence and majesty?

But what is the arm of the Lord really like? Verse 2, 'He grew up before him like a tender shoot, and like a root out of a dry ground.' Jesus is the shoot of the root of Jesse. He was born and grew up like any child and from a human point of view he was just like any other young shoot. He was planted in inhospitable parched soil, remember those early stories? Born in obscurity and poverty, cradled in a manger, fleeing as a refugee to Egypt, rescued eventually from Egypt by the Word of God, then reared in a non-descript Galilean village. It wasn't very hospitable ground for the shoot to grow up in! Is that how the Lord reveals his mighty arm? It is an amazing strategy!

And as he grows to maturity no one takes a second look at him. Verse 2, 'he had no beauty or majesty to attract us to him, nothing in his appearance that we should desire him.' As Jesus was growing up in Nazareth he has no majestic presence, no personal charisma, no film star looks, none of the trappings of celebrity, none of the things that our culture thinks are important, but then that's always God's way isn't it? Look at verse 3, twice we are told he was despised. And that echoes through the gospels doesn't it? Contempt and rejection from religious leaders and his contemporaries, culminating in the mockery of a trial, the ignominy and shame of a public and appallingly painful death on the cross. They all turned their backs on him, they hid their faces from him. It's as though he was thrown on the garbage heap. 'He was a man of suffering', literally he knew grief and suffering as a close friend. Even his disciples forsook him and fled.

But I want you to notice at the end of verse 3, there is a new dimension introduced by that little word 'we'. He was despised and 'we held him in low esteem.' That stands for the whole of humanity. There was a time in every one of our lives – it may have been very early on, before we first came to faith and as children we hardly remember when we didn't trust Jesus, but for many of us it was a much longer period, when we held him in low esteem. Maybe we admired his teaching and nodded agreement to his values but when we see him dying there to rescue me from my sins, which will otherwise condemn me to hell, then we start, naturally because of our human and fallen nature, to turn away. And people still criticize this gospel of the cross don't they? And even in the church the cross sometimes becomes an embarrassment because, of course, it is much easier to preach a message that offers all the blessings of the kingdom without any real repentance or humbling of ourselves before God.

It is so easy for us to take a gospel we would like to hear and to substitute that for the true gospel. It's one thing to wear a cross as a chain around your neck, it's another to have the cross ruling in your heart. That's a very different matter! So people say to me, 'When I was a child or a young person I was into evangelism, the gospel and the cross . . . I've moved on from there now.' What have you moved on to? There is only one place to move on to from the cross and that is heaven! Don't move from the cross, there is no other saving power.

Evangelism has become so focused on making things as easy as possible for people to accept the idea of God. But friends, the real question is not whether I can accept God, but whether there is any way in which God could accept me? He is the holy, holy, holy God and without the man of sorrows you are left with a man-made, me-centred, sentimental religion that aims for the feel-good factor, and nobody is going to be saved by that, nobody is going to sacrifice or suffer for that. As soon as the going gets tough those adherents will just pack up and go! It's a big danger in our culture to want Jesus Christ as a sort of superstar who will take us up to his orbit, shower us with blessings and expect nothing from us. But the man of sorrows says,

> Whoever wants to be my disciple must deny themselves and take up their cross and follow me. For whoever wants to save their life will lose it, but whoever loses their life for me and the gospel will save it.
> (Mark 8:34–35)

That's the Jesus we meet in Isaiah. Are we going to hide our faces?

So we come to the central stanza of the poem, verses 4–6. And here my question is: What will he do? I phrase it in the present tense but you see that the poem puts it in the past tense because of the certainty of what he is going to accomplish.

There is a familiar argument, 'there is no smoke without fire'. And people said it while Jesus was on the cross and have said it ever since, 'If he is suffering so appallingly he must be a great sinner.' The religious leaders saw the cross as God's righteous judgment on Jesus' blasphemy because he called himself the Son of God. They were right that he was suffering a divine punishment but they were totally wrong as to the reason for that punishment. In verse 4 it suddenly becomes clear, he is suffering our punishment. He is lifting up our griefs; he is carrying away our sorrows. We were right to esteem him as smitten by God, but that is because he is carrying the curse and dying on the cross for us, who deserve to be smitten by God.

Verse 5, carries us to the very heart of the matter, as it moves beyond our sorrow and grief, to our sins: 'He was pierced for our transgressions, he was crushed for our iniquities.' Transgressions, as you probably know, means crossing a line, wilful rebellion through disobedience. Iniquity refers to the stain on our consciousness, the inerasable effect of sin, our inner fallen nature. And so, the Lord Jesus died because of our sins and our rebellion. And that is the 'great exchange' Martin Luther spoke about from 2 Corinthians 5 when Jesus takes our chastisement, our stripes, the punishment that we so justly deserve and in its place we have peace, salvation, shalom, the rightness with God that we could never produce ourselves.[3]

So the servant willingly identifies with our sinful condition and – by his death, in our place, as our substitute – we enter into life. Now this is the heart of the good news, this is the gospel of grace. The central doctrine of our faith is the substitutionary atonement of Jesus Christ for our sins. That doesn't exhaust everything you could say about the cross and the resurrection of Jesus but it is the basic biblical understanding and without it any other perspective is devoid of real meaning. This is not just a theory of atonement as some theologians would say, it is not just one model among many. At the heart of biblical Christianity is the atoning death of Jesus in our place, a death that involves him bearing the penalty for our sin. And at that point the big question of Isaiah is answered, the enigma is solved – this is God's servant, his Son, total and sufficient in himself, absolute righteousness and purity, answering our human dilemma. It's all of God, it's all of grace and that is why the gospel is such good news. That little word 'for' in verse 5, he did it '*for* our transgressions . . . *for* our iniquities', means 'on behalf of', 'arising out of', 'because of us'. The servant carried the righteous sentence of God's wrath against sin, in our place, as our substitute. He was forsaken so that we might be forgiven.

So back to our passage, verse 6 summarizes it beautifully. Do you see how verse 6 begins with 'all' and ends with 'all'? 'We *all*, like sheep, have gone astray . . . and the Lord has laid on him the iniquity of us *all*.' Now a straying sheep has no provision for food beyond the grazing it can find. Certainly in the Middle East, it needed to be led by the waters and green pastures, it has no projection from danger, no company, no comfort. A straying sheep is a picture of being lost, solitary, miserable and under the threat of death and 'we all, like sheep, have gone astray.' By nature and by behaviour we are alienated and cut off from God, that's the human condition. We are born into it, we confirm it and extend it by our choices day by day. But the glory of this passage is that the straying sheep is saved by the sacrificial lamb. This is the Lord's initiative, it is his will; it is his way. The covenant God steps in in his grace and faithfulness and lays the iniquity of us all on Jesus. I love that last part of verse 6, it's as though God goes around looking for all our iniquities, gathers them all up, and he puts them on to the head and shoulders of the Lord Jesus as he hangs on that cross. The cross says that God could not possibly love you more than he does, and he will never love you less. And we respond with Horatio Spafford:

> My sin, oh, the bliss of this glorious thought!
> My sin not in part, but the whole,
> Is nailed to his cross and I bear it no more,
> Praise the Lord, praise the Lord, oh my soul![4]

Question four, how has he done it? Verses 7–9 give the answer. We move back from explanation in verses 4–6 to description in 7–9. Here Isaiah emphasizes not just that Christ's suffering was vicarious but voluntary. He allowed himself to be afflicted and oppressed, he accepted it like a sheep about to be slaughtered (verse 7). He could have called for legions of angels to deliver him in an instant. If you've ever visited the Garden of Gethsemane you will know that he had only to climb the hill for another ten minutes and he'd be out into the Judean wilderness, lost in the night. He could have so easily slipped away but he didn't run or resist. He didn't revile or retaliate, he chose to endure it all for us. At the very peak of his life, in his early thirties, his life was snuffed out because he willed it to be so for the transgressions of his people.

He died, crucified between thieves, surrounded by the taunts and mockery of evil men. But his grave was not Gehenna, the rubbish tip outside the city of Jerusalem where the bodies of crucified victims were usually thrown. No, he was buried in the tomb of a rich man, Joseph of Arimathea. Once the suffering was over his privileged burial was elegant testimony to his innocence and his vindication by his Father. And, of course, it was the evidence on which the resurrection was to be based: the empty tomb and the risen Lord. How has he done it? By that self-sacrificing love and mercy.

And so lastly, verses 10–12, what is the outcome? I want you to see that the beginning of verse 10 is tremendously significant, 'It was the Lord's will to crush him.' The death of our Lord Jesus was not ultimately at the hands of wicked men but in the hands of the Lord. Now remember, the Lord is the holy Trinity: Father, Son and Holy Spirit, from eternity to eternity. The Father sent the Son to be the

Saviour of the world, but the Son was not a reluctant victim. In the foreknowledge and counsel of God he decrees that God, in a human body, will die for our sins. 'Crush' is a very strong verb, it means to grind down; his very self became a guilt offering for us.

When his soul makes an offering for sin then he shall see his offspring. Once that offering had been made then the future was opened up to an entirely different scenario. I love the idea that the Hebrew word for offering comes from the verb meaning 'to draw near'. An offering is that which draws you near, which brings you near to God. What is it that brings you near to God? The Lord Jesus giving himself as the sin offering for us sinners. Isaiah experienced this, in a measure, back in chapter 6 when his own guilt was taken away and his sin was purged because the coal came from the altar, from the place of sacrifice. But now, on a universal and eternal scale, that sort of cleansing is available to the people of God.

This opens the door to a new world, which is what the end of verse 10 is foreshadowing. The straying sheep now become children. They are given new life; they are offspring of the Saviour himself. And verse 11 makes it even clearer, out of the anguish of his soul he will be satisfied. Even here in this prophecy, seven hundred years before the cross, there is life, resurrection, and vitality. The servant has come through death and now he is alive for evermore. And he looks back, not with regret, but with satisfaction.

And moving to the New Testament we can say the Lord Jesus sees his church – a stream of men and women from every nation redeemed though his blood – made righteous through this great exchange, with their iniquities removed as far as the east is from the west. We are ransomed, healed, restored, and forgiven. And it's through knowing him, the Righteous One, that we are counted righteous. His righteousness is put to our account and as he works that righteousness out in progressive holiness we become more like Jesus.

The song, in verse 12, adds the final piece of the jigsaw as it celebrates the limitless victory which Jesus' sacrifice has achieved. No conquest in world history is greater than the victory of our Lord Jesus Christ. So the servant lives on as a conquering king. The imagery of this verse sees him enjoying the spoils of his victory in the God-given priorities of his exaltation and his ascension on high to the right-hand of the Father. And so he pours out his grace on his people as the fruit of his passion and as he ascends to heaven the choirs around the throne are singing, 'Worthy is the Lamb, who was slain!' (Revelation 5:12).

May I ask you, do you belong to the Lord Jesus? Can you say, 'Jesus died for me'? Have you put your faith in him? Have you put your hand in his hand, the hand of the Good Shepherd, for time and for eternity? Well if you have, rejoice in the victory of Calvary! He has overcome the sharpness of death; he has conquered all the hostile forces that were ranged against us, even the devil himself. He has robbed death of its sting and he has opened the everlasting kingdom of heaven to all believers, yes, *all* believers, 'for the Lord has laid on him the iniquity of us *all*' (verse 6).

So my friends, the rescue is complete. When Jesus did that great work his final cry was, 'Finished'. The gospel writers tell us that the moment the sacrifice was complete the temple curtain was torn in two, from the top to the bottom (Matthew 27:51). No human hand could tear it, it was far too thick, but God wrenches down the curtain by an act of his own grace and love in the death of his Son. And he says to all the world, Jews and Gentiles, 'You can come in now. The way to my presence is open. You are no longer far off. I've brought you near in the blood of Christ. Jews and Gentiles, slaves and free, male and female – you are all one in this Lord Jesus. Behold my Servant.'

Notes

1. W. Y. Fullerton, *Charles Spurgeon: A Biography: The Life of C. H. Spurgeon by a Close Friend* (CreateSpace Independent Publishing Platform, 2014).
2. Philip Bliss, 'Man of sorrows', 1875.
3. Martin Luther, *Werke* (Weimar, 1883), 5: 608.
4. Horatio Spafford, 'It is well with my soul', 1873.

Other Addresses

What Does It Mean to Be Filled with the Spirit?

by Derek Tidball

Derek Tidball is a Baptist Minister who has spent much of his life in theological education. Formerly Principal of London School of Theology he now teaches in various colleges including Spurgeon's, Moorlands and SAIACS (Bangalore). Derek has authored many books including *The Message of Leviticus* in the BST series. His latest book, *The Voices of the New Testament* (IVP), is an innovative approach to New Testament theology. He has also written this year's Keswick Study Guide, *Transformed: Becoming like God's Son.* Derek is married to Dianne, a Baptist Regional Minister.

What Does It Mean to Be Filled with the Spirit? Galatians 5:16–26

One cold day in 1946 a young and not very exceptional preacher was closeted in a hotel room in Pontypridd with the British preacher Stephen Olford. On their second day together, Olford spoke of how God had completely turned his life inside out through his experiencing the fullness and anointing of the Holy Spirit. Olford explained the fullness of the Holy Spirit was available to every believer who was willing to bow daily and hourly to the sovereignty of Christ and to the authority of his Word. The young evangelist and the mature preacher then sought God fervently, like Jacob laying hold of God, until they came to a point of rest and praise. The young evangelist spoke of it as a turning point in his life that would revolutionize his ministry. And it did. His name was Billy Graham.[1]

Tonight could be the turning point in your life and service for God. There is no better guide to what it means to be filled with the Holy Spirit than Paul in Galatians 5:16–26. Through four chapters he has battled with the Galatians to explain that the only way to be justified before God is to have faith in Christ. Their works and their obedience to the law were dead ends that would never be sufficient to make them right with God. But now, he explains, the justified believer is also the Spirit-filled believer. Justification – God's verdict of 'not guilty' pronounced on undeserving sinners – cannot lead to the living of self-centred lives of licentious indulgence. Authentic justification must lead to Christ-centred lives of service in which we are being transformed by the power of the Holy Spirit.

1. He speaks of being led by the Spirit (verses 16–18)

In this section of his letter Paul starts by explaining what it means to be led by the Spirit. Believers are to be led by the Spirit as soldiers lead their prisoners to captivity and farmers lead their cattle for milking. We follow him as he goes ahead of us, determining the route and making the decisions which we follow, whenever we face a choice as to how to live.

To be led by the Spirit involves a threefold calling. First, *it is a call to action*, verse 16. Paul chooses his words carefully and says not so much 'Live by the Spirit' as 'Walk by the Spirit'. He's tapping into the long-standing Jewish vocabulary which sets out our moral and ethical obligation before God, hence, the way we live. The prophet Hosea declared, 'The ways of the Lord are right, the righteous walk in them' (Hosea 14:9). The prophet Micah looked forward to the time when other nations would come to the Jerusalem Temple and ask God to 'teach us his ways, so that we might walk in his paths' (Micah 4:2). Christian believers equally have an obligation to walk in the ways of the Lord, but this way is not the path of the law but the path of faith. Hence the call is accompanied by a promise, live by the Spirit, 'and you will not gratify the desires of the flesh' (verse 16).

There is no place for spiritual couch potatoes. The Spirit does not come upon the lazy or inactive. We do not enter the fullness of the Spirit by indolent passivity, although, as the Sovereign Lord, the Spirit is quite capable of invading our lives uninvited. But rather than challenging him to do so, we need to get off the spiritual couch and put one step in front of another in obedience. I like the story of the man who advertised in the *Los Angeles Times* that if people paid him he would jog on their behalf and go to the gym for them and at the end of the month would transfer to them the benefits he had gained – the weight loss, the greater fitness and the increased sense of well-being. He's my kind of guy! The trouble is it doesn't work like that. And we can't be filled with the Spirit by proxy, any more that we can get physically fit by proxy. To be filled with the Spirit requires us to personally be active and to 'walk by the Spirit'.

Secondly, *it is a call to battle*, verse 17. The moment we step off the couch we step into the battlefield. We quickly realize that there are two very different frames of mind, two totally different dispositions we can adopt in life, that are not only irreconcilable but are at war with each other. 'The flesh desires what is contrary to the Spirit and the Spirit what is contrary to the flesh. They are in conflict with each other.'

Do not be misled by this language into thinking that the battle between the flesh and the Spirit is a battle between the material and the spiritual, the physical and other-worldly piety. We do not have to escape life in the everyday real world in order to be spiritual; we do not have to have some mystical out-of-body experience to be full of the Spirit. New Testament spirituality is always an embodied spirituality, about life in the here-and-now, even as we prepare for the life to come. When Paul speaks of flesh he is not talking about our physical make-up but rather our human weakness, our corruptibility, our liability to give in to temptation, our sinfulness.

The wellspring of this is 'desire' which he mentions in verses 16 and 17. In itself desire might be neutral, we might desire something good as well as something bad. But given our fallen natures, our desires are often bent towards to the wrong things. When I am confronted by a lettuce leaf or a cream cake, I know where my desire is going to take me! Desires are often impulsive, expressing a deeply rooted tendency to focus on ourselves and what we want rather than what is right before God.

The truth is we will never be free from this battle until we are finally transformed in the presence of God. J. C. Ryle was right: 'He that would understand the nature of holiness must know that the Christian is a "man of war". If we would be holy, we must fight. The true Christian is called to be a soldier and must behave as such from the day of his conversion to the day of his death.'[2] With disturbing candour, Ryle confessed, 'Even after conversion he (the Christian) carries within him a nature prone to evil, and a heart weak and unstable as water.'[3]

Thirdly, *it is a call to surrender*, verse 18. We must stand in defiance against 'the desires of the flesh', crying out, 'no surrender'. We must never give up the fight against our enemy on that front. But there is one to whom we must surrender. To be led by the Spirit is to yield ourselves to his authority and therefore to open ourselves to the empowerment of God himself in the battle against sin. We can conquer if we surrender to the Spirit and allow him to lead. I know the sad truth of this in my own experience that when I take back control of my own life, the desires of the flesh get the upper hand. Daily, hourly surrender is needed.

2. He speaks of living contrary to the Spirit (verses 19–21)

Just in case we should be in any doubt, Paul now focuses in on 'the acts of the flesh'. His technique is rather like one of those maps where a certain section of it is pulled out, reproduced on a large scale and put in a circle for clarification.

Remember these are 'acts of the flesh' not because they are physical but because they express our ugly, unrestrained, natural human weaknesses and are a denial of all that the Spirit of God would produce in us. Here is humanity, not as God intended but humanity turned in on itself. It has become customary to justify several patterns of sinful behaviour on the basis of, 'that's the way God made us'. But to claim that about lifestyles which are clearly contrary to God's ways is not only to fail to recognize the impact of the fall on our make-up but also to throw what God made to be good, and designed to be kept good, back in his face.

Here is a dreadful catalogue of sin, covering the whole range of life. It deals with outward actions and inner attitudes. It deals with sins that particularly characterized the Jews, and those that they particularly associated with the Gentiles, such as idolatry. It deals with sins in the sexual, religious, emotional and social dimensions of life.

Sexual sins are listed in verse 19, namely, 'immorality', which is promiscuity and using God's good gifts how we like rather than how he has determined; 'impurity', which takes us inwards to the way we think; and, 'debauchery', which is sexual excess.

Religious sins, listed in verse 20, include 'idolatry'. This was especially characteristic of the Gentiles and included not only the visible representation of the gods but anything which became the object of worship, even things which in themselves might be good like family or sport but when distorted, become ends in themselves and spiritual liabilities. To this he adds 'witchcraft', a term which represents a whole raft of practices associated with contacting the unseen spiritual world and trying to manipulate it to our own ends.

So far, Keswick regulars may feel they are on safe ground. They'd run a mile at any suggestion of such 'acts of the flesh'. But we may find ourselves in the crosshairs when it comes to the next category, that of *emotional sins*. These include both actions and attitudes that destroy fellowship, sometimes divide churches, and distance others from us. They are 'hatred, discord, jealousy, fits of rage, selfish ambition'. It is possible, of course, to feel them inside without expressing them outwardly. We may be good at the game of 'cover-up spirituality'. But that's no less an act of the flesh.

Lastly, there are *social sins*, mentioned in the last half of verse 20 and verse 21. With 'drunkenness' and 'orgies' he seems to be back where he started, but then, uncomfortably for many, he also includes 'dissensions, factions and envy'. Some churches may suffer from sexual excess and drunkenness, but many more suffer from divisions, factions and envy. It's possible, of course, to dress them up in the name of spiritual passion, doctrinal purity or protecting the truth. Dissension and factionalism are often carried out in the name of the gospel or the Holy Spirit. We can sometimes be driven by a cause rather than by grace and divide the church. This may be an issue of which you need to repent, right now. Whatever the motive, Paul names and condemns them as 'acts of the flesh' that are at war with the work of the Spirit within us. We need to hear the words of Richard Baxter on the unity of the church in which, to paraphrase, he warned 'we need to be very suspicious of religious passions and distinguish carefully between a sound and sinful zeal in case we blame the Holy Spirit for giving to sin and are deluded into thinking that we are most pleasing to God when we are actually most offending him.'[4]

Having set out the dreadful catalogue of the acts of the flesh, Paul now briefly speaks of the dreadful end to which such acts lead, 'Those who live like this will not inherit the Kingdom of God' (verse 21). Such lifestyles lead to a catastrophic dead end, like a train hitting the buffers at speed. Those who live like this have no part in the renewed creation where God will reign over all in perfect harmony.

3. He speaks of being filled with the Spirit (verses 22–26)

To be filled with the Spirit means three things. Firstly, *we exhibit the Spirit's fruit*, verses 22–23. In contrast to the *works* of the flesh, Paul turns to the *fruit* of the Spirit. The one is mechanical, the other is organic. We manufacture the one, the Spirit produces the other. The Spirit has taken up residence in every believer and if he is given the run of the house the evidence of his living within will soon be evident. Think of when you brought your newborn baby home from hospital. Their presence soon affected your lifestyle and living quarters. You could no longer do as you chose. You decorated the nursery. You were prepared for the sleepless nights, and for sick to go down your clothes. But you also witnessed the miracle and knew the joy of seeing a life develop. So when the Spirit resides within, unless he is neglected or confined to a tiny part of the house, the signs of his residence will soon be evident.

Fruit, as we know, takes time to grow. It doesn't happen overnight. Sometimes it involves painful pruning. So don't be discouraged if you haven't produced that perfect supermarket quality fruit in your life yet. Don't give up. Allow the master gardener, the master pruner, to do his work.

You'll be familiar with the fruit – nine different kinds of it. 'Love' is the primary, all-encompassing grace, which isn't about a funny feeling in the stomach or a flutter of the heart but is an active quality of self-sacrifice for others. 'Joy' is not enforced jollity or superficial cheerfulness that is liable to change with the weather. It is that uncontrived expression of deep trust in God which gives rise to thankfulness and the delight that comes from knowing that God's in charge and he can be trusted. It expresses itself in all sorts of ways. Some of us are more extrovert than others. Don't measure the genuineness of someone's joy by whether they dance or swing from the chandeliers! Emotions are not always best judged by outward expression.

'Peace' must not be reduced to individualistic inner tranquillity but is about seeking the well-being of others and working for harmonious relationships with them.

'Forbearance' or patience, which is long-temperedness, is named as a quality belonging to God himself in Romans 2:4, as is the next quality. 'Kindness' and 'goodness' go together. Kindness errs on the side of our disposition whereas goodness errs on the side of activity. It's kindness in action. At its heart it means to be generous.

'Faithfulness' refers to loyalty, integrity, and commitment to God, his truth, and to our fellow believers. 'Gentleness' was despised in the Greek world, as it often is today. We treasure forcefulness and strength. Gentleness, though, is never to be mistaken for spinelessness but, to be precise, it is meekness, a word which is used of the breaking in of a horse. The strength remains and isn't diminished but it is channelled constructively and not exhibited chaotically or destructively. Lastly there is 'self-control', which takes us back to the question of desire. Self-control is about mastering one's desires, in the strength of the Spirit, rather than being mastered by them.

This remarkable basket of fruit is composed of nine different kinds, but they all belong together. The picture is rather like one of those blended fruit juices where you can detect the peach, mango, apple, and pear which go to make up the one rich harmonious mixture. Except, this is not extracted juice, but the real thing. The image is of a fruit basket where all the fruit needs to be displayed. It's not a box of chocolates where you can select your favourite and leave the ones you don't like untouched for others to eat. We can't specialize in some of the fruit and leave the rest to others. We cannot say we specialize in joy and so excuse ourselves from lacking patience with those who struggle with depression. We cannot say we're wonderfully self-disciplined, and pride ourselves on disregarding those who aren't. We must aim for peace with them and show kindness and patience towards them.

We may naturally tend towards some fruit rather than others but they check each other in order to form a perfect balance in our characters. We have to let the Spirit cultivate those areas where we are weakest. What a wonderful picture of a Christlike character this gives. Don't you long to be like this? As Paul says, 'There's no law that opposes things like that',[5] but there's no law that can produce it either. For that, we have to follow a different route, to which Paul now turns.

To be filled with the Spirit means, secondly, *we die the Saviour's death*, verse 24. The sudden mention of crucifixion here seems to jar with the pleasant image of the Holy Spirit producing tasty and healthy fruit in our lives. We are jerked from thinking of idyllic orchards and prolific vineyards to the awful, brutal and horrific scene of execution. But the cross is at the heart of it all, not only as the most significant fact of history and the means of our salvation, but as a significant element of our present experience of the Spirit. 'Those who belong to Christ Jesus have crucified the flesh with its passions and desires' (verse 24). In surrendering our lives to be led by the Spirit we have killed off those compulsions to sin.

Crucifixion is a decisive act. The person crucified dies. Paul highlights that by saying, 'those who belong to Christ have crucified the flesh.' But crucifixion is also a process. The person crucified takes time to die. It's not like being shot, or beheaded. The victim is strung up on a cross until life expires. Sometimes it took days to die. So, by definition, by constitution, we are dead people, crucified with Christ. And yet we need to go on dying daily, to renew that commitment to decisively reject those impulses to live self-centred lives governed by the flesh.

The key point is this. The road to being filled with the Spirit unavoidably takes us through the road of the cross. Tom Smail, one of the leaders of the charismatic movement a few years back, writes movingly of how he discovered this in his early days of renewal: 'There is no way to Pentecost except by Calvary; the Spirit is given by the Cross.'[6] 'The Holy Spirit's function,' he points out, 'is to reflect in us the likeness of Christ . . . but how could he do that with any authenticity . . . if he did not also lead us into the likeness of his suffering.'[7] To be filled with the Spirit requires that we go to the cross, not to stand at its foot and wonder at it but to mount it ourselves and die on it to our old sinful ways of living. Are we prepared to pay the price?

Thirdly, to be filled with the Spirit means *we march in the Spirit's army*, verses 25–26. Paul sums it all up with the exhortation to 'keep in step with the Spirit'. But we should note that in speaking like this he's using military language. We're called to walk in step with the Spirit as individuals, but equally to keep in step as we march in the Lord's army with ranks upon ranks of other soldiers of Christ, serving our Commander.

He immediately explains that we keep in step by not becoming 'conceited, provoking and envying each other.' Being superior to others, competing with others and being jealous is the quickest way to cause chaos in the ranks and destroy the army's progress. It means we set off with the right foot while everyone else starts with the left. It means we're marching to a different tempo than the rest of the army, either too quick or too slow. The infantry's formation is destroyed and no longer under the command of its General. To keep in step with the Spirit is as much about learning to walk under his direction together as it is about cultivating any personal Christlike qualities.

So there we have it. Paul uses four verbs to tell us how to be filled with the Spirit. First we must *walk by the Spirit*, actively seeking him and following his ways. Secondly, we must be *led by the Spirit*, completely surrendering to his control. Thirdly, we must *live by the Spirit*, crucifying self to allow his fruit-bearing presence to change us. Fourthly, we must *keep in step with the Spirit*, serving Christ with others under his command.

This could be the night when you take that step of being serious about surrendering to the Holy Spirit – the turning point of your life and of your service for Christ. Will you commit yourself from this moment on, to be led by the Spirit?

Notes

1. John Pollock, *Billy Graham* (Hodder & Stoughton, 1966), pp. 62–63.
2. J. C. Ryle, *Holiness* (James Clark, 1956 reprint), pp. 51–52.
3. Ibid., p. 53.
4. Richard Baxter, *The Cure of Church Divisions* (1670), Clause 20.
5. Tom Wright's translation of Galatians 5:23, *The New Testament for Everyone* (SPCK, 2011).
6. Thomas Smail, *Reflected Glory: The Spirit in Christ and Christians* (Hodder & Stoughton, 1975), p. 105.
7. Ibid., p. 112.

Eternity Is at Stake

by Rico Tice

Rico Tice is the Senior Minister (Evangelism) at All Souls, Langham Place in London. Joining in 1994 during the later years of the ministry of John Stott, his main role is to help the hundreds of enquirers about the Christian faith who come through the doors of the church each year. He has also developed the Christianity Explored course, which introduces people to Jesus through studying the Gospel of Mark. Other than rugby, Rico's hobbies include playing golf and watching films. He married Lucy in December 2008 and they have three young children, Peter, Daniel and Mercy.

Eternity Is at Stake: Mark 9:42–50

Well, I'd like to begin this evening with a little bit of a Keswick quiz. I'm going to give you four names, then read two quotations and I'd like you to identify the author of the quotes. So, the four names are Pharaoh, the Emperor Nero, Muhammad and Adolf Hitler. Which of these men said the following? Quote one, 'Throw these worthless servants into the darkness, they can weep there and grind their teeth.' Quote two, 'Get out of my presence you damned, and go to the fire that will burn for ever.' Well, of course, it's a trick question. The answer is, 'none of the above'. The person who said both of those things is our Lord Jesus Christ, the most loving man that ever lived, who, in the Sermon on the Mount said, 'Love your enemies and pray for those who persecute you' (Matthew 5:44). Even as he was being murdered he cried out for his killers,

'Father, forgive them, for they don't know what they are doing!' (Luke 23:34). And this evening we are going to be speaking about hell and Jesus is equally unequivocal in Mark 9:47–48:

> And if your eye causes you to stumble, pluck it out. It is better for you to enter the kingdom of God with one eye than to have two eyes and be thrown into hell, where 'the worms that eat them do not die, and the fire is not quenched.'

The subject of hell is scarcely raised within much of the church today. I heard this story on good authority from Sinclair Ferguson, a Christian minister I absolutely trust. A member of the royal family was leaving one of the great worship centres of England and said to the presiding minister, a figure of some significance in the hierarchy of the church, 'Is it true that there is a hell?' The minister replied, 'Your highness, Jesus taught so, the church has always believed so and the creeds teach so.' And the reply he got was this, 'Then why in the name of God will you not say so?'

Why is it that we won't be honest? Well, there are many reasons. We don't want to lose friendships. There is a pain line to cross; you can feel the butterflies as you hit it. And actually the very mention of the word 'hell' in a worship service causes a sharp intake of breath. It's not a subject of polite conversation. In fact, I know of no subject that would be less appreciated. Indeed, the only contexts in which the word may be used without feathers being ruffled is as a joke or a curse, 'Where the hell are my car keys?'

But 'hell' is a word that runs right through the Bible. And you cannot fully appreciate the coming of Jesus Christ without grasping what the Bible says about hell. Just as in a great painting it is often the dark backdrop that makes the foreground appear so luminous and shine with such clarity, so it is only when we plumb the dark depths of our human destiny that the wonder of God's love and grace appear as the amazing provision they are. To be convinced you are loved you need to see the extent of the rescue, the horror of your sin. And the gospel does that as we see the wonder of salvation set against the dark depths of our own need and sinfulness. So we cannot fully appreciate what it means to be raised up to the promise of heaven unless we realize that we are raised up there from the prospect of hell.

Now again, I don't know where your heart is now, but mine is weary. This is a subject of great sadness because I come from a family where I have many relatives who conduct their lives convinced that these solemn truths are untrue, or if they are true they are somehow irrelevant. It's not just me is it? And I want to ask and try to answer some crucial questions about the subject of hell and explain why it is so vitally important for us as Christians, and more especially if you are not a Christian.

So question one, does hell really exist? Paul the apostle tells us in 2 Timothy 1:10 about 'the appearing of our

Saviour, Jesus Christ, who has destroyed death and has brought life and immortality to light through the gospel.' Here is Paul, about to be executed, writing to young Timothy, and he cries out with days left to live, 'Jesus Christ has destroyed death.' In other words, by his death on Good Friday and his resurrection on Easter Day, Jesus has secured for us eternal life. He was tried in a Roman and Jewish Court and he was sentenced to die. They strung him on a cross, they put a spear through his side, they took him off the cross and certified him dead and three days later he was walking around again.

He got through death himself, he can get me through. Therefore the proper epitaph to write for the Christian is not 'Rest In Peace', RIP, but CAD, 'Christ Abolished Death'. We are CADs. The resurrection is the proof that Christ holds the future, that past certainty gives me a future hope. Five years ago I was with my mother as she died in Basingstoke hospital. I loved her very much and as I sat with her I said three things to her. I said, 'goodbye' – we'd all say that. I said, 'I love you' – we'd all say that. And then I said, 'I'll see you again', and that is because Christ has risen. It is an amazing thing to know that because of him you will put your arms around loved ones again, if they trusted in him. And so, we look to the Lord Jesus and ask the question, 'What do you say, Lord Jesus, about life and death?' And he not only makes heaven and the new creation real, clear and assured by his resurrection; he also by his resurrection, supremely in the pages in the New Testament, speaks of the reality of hell.

The one who most clearly and most fully teaches about the fact of hell is none other than the Lord Jesus Christ. Now I want you to flick through some of Jesus' words in Matthew's Gospel. I want you to come with me and get up close and personal to Jesus. Ask yourself, are you familiar with this man? Is this man preached in your church?

Matthew 5:22: 'Anyone who says, "You fool!" will be in danger of the fire of hell.'

Matthew 5:29: 'If your right eye causes you to stumble, gouge it out and throw it away. It is better for you to lose one part of your body than for your whole body to be thrown into hell.'

Matthew 7:13: 'Enter through the narrow gate. For wide is the gate and broad is the road that leads to destruction, and many enter through it.'

On we go . . .

Matthew 8:12: 'But the subjects of the kingdom will be thrown outside, into the darkness, where there will be weeping and gnashing of teeth.'

Matthew 10:28: 'Do not be afraid of those who kill the body but cannot kill the soul. Rather, be afraid of the One who can destroy both soul and body in hell.'

Matthew 13:42: 'They will throw them into the blazing furnace, where there will be weeping and gnashing of teeth.'

Matthew 13:50: 'Throw them into the blazing furnace.'

Matthew 18:8, our verse again from Mark chapter 9, 'If your hand or foot causes you to stumble, cut it off and throw it away. It is better for you to enter life maimed or crippled than to have two hands or two feet and be thrown into eternal fire.'

This is Jesus Christ, up close and personal. And I need to ask you, are you familiar with him? For those people who say, 'O, I love the Sermon on the Mount, I believe every word of it!' Really? Do you see what he says here? Please see the theme here – there is judgment leading to condemnation, leading to conditions variously described as weeping, loss, gnashing of teeth or flames of fire. Why does he use such vivid language? Loving Jesus, passionate Jesus, caring Jesus, life-transforming Jesus – why does he of all people not keep silent? Why? Because this is the very reason he came to the world. Because unless he came to die the destiny that awaits men and women, that awaits us, is beyond thinking, beyond bearing. And here is the issue, please hear this: this is the only Jesus there is. If this isn't Jesus then we have no idea who Jesus was. This is the Jesus who came to save sinners, who gave himself. We need to understand this to see the salvation he brings because, without him, our destiny is one of infinite loss.

In December 1984 there was a huge fog on the M25 motorway and early in the morning a lorry carrying paper crashed in the fog. All the warning lights were on, the hazard signs were out, and the police arrived on the scene very quickly. But driver after driver ignored the warning lights, ignored the hazard signs, ignored the fog and drove on. Apparently a policeman, realizing what was happening, became so possessed with fear about the destruction he was seeing, so desperate to stop more people dying, that he actually picked up traffic cones and threw them at the windscreens of the oncoming cars. One newspaper report read as follows, 'One of the policemen had tears running down his face because he threw cones and people would pay no attention.' Desperate picture, isn't it? In this passage and so many others in Matthew Jesus throws cones at the window screen. He says, 'Please hear me, this is real!' He could not be more vivid in his language. The one raised from the dead tells us that hell exists.

So question one, is hell real? Yes, Jesus says so. Question two, what then is hell like? Many of us Christians say, 'Well, it's something the Bible speaks so little about that anything I said would be speculative.' The truth of the matter is almost the reverse! The Bible has metres, yards, on the nature of hell. Granted the Bible understands that the reality of hell is so terrible that it must go beyond the power of human language to either explain or describe it, but it does have several important things to say about the nature of hell. It says the following things. One, it is a sphere of punishment. The whole function of Jesus' teaching is to underscore for us that there is a just judgment of God in which men and women are separated from his presence as a penal judgment for their rejection of God's authority and their rejection of Jesus Christ. These men that say to him, 'I will not be a tenant in your world, I will be the owner, I am pushing away your Son.' And the kind of language Jesus uses is that of one who experiences punishment: Mark 9:48, 'The worms that eat them do not die, and the fire is not quenched.'

Two, it is a sphere of separation, of outer darkness. Living in London, as I do, I can't imagine this total darkness. But come to the hills and mountains around Keswick, find somewhere really remote, and on a cloudy night you can put your hand right in front of your face and not see it. That is the level of darkness. And Jesus says, in hell you will be totally isolated, alone, disoriented and above all separated from the relationships that give you your identity, your value, your sense of function. So this is total separation and Jesus is hurling that traffic cone at your front window. He says, 'Believe me!'

And perhaps the most solemn thing about all this is how our Lord Jesus uses the word 'everlasting'. You see, disorientation we can take for a moment, punishment we can endure for a season, separation we could cope with if we knew it was going to end, but the horror of this situation is that it is eternal or everlasting. Matthew 25:46, 'Then they will go away to eternal punishment, but the righteous to eternal life.' In that verse the word for 'eternal life' is the same word as 'eternal punishment'. Eternal.

Now what does this say to us? It says to us that God takes your life with infinite seriousness. He takes your relationship to him with infinite seriousness and, on this occasion, I mean *infinite*. If we reject that relationship then we reject him who is life and the source of life. And, in a strange way, he dignifies us by saying, 'I will take your decision about your relationship with me with permanent seriousness.'

So is hell real? Yes. What is it like? It is a place of suffering. Question three, who is it for? Well verses 43–47 make that clear:

> If your hand causes you to stumble, cut it off. It is better for you to enter life maimed than with two hands to go into hell, where the fire never goes out. And if your foot causes you to stumble, cut it off. It is better for you to enter life crippled than to have two feet and be thrown into hell. And if your eye causes you to stumble, pluck it out. It is better for you to enter the kingdom of God with one eye than to have two eyes and be thrown into hell.

Hell is for people who say, 'Listen, nobody tells me what I do with my hands. I am an individualist. No one tells me where my feet can go, my feet will go wherever I like. No one tells me what I can and can't look at.' The road to destruction in Matthew 7 is full of people who say, 'I can think as I please' and 'I can do as I please'. But God says, 'What you do with the hands I have wonderfully made, what you do with the feet I've made, what you do with the extraordinary eyes that I have made is my, the Creator's, business.' How I treat you matters to God, how you treat me matters to God, and how we treat the world matters to God. So there is a choice here – kill sin or be killed by it. I can either say, 'No one can tell me how to live' and that sin cuts me off from the God who made me and gave me so many gifts and it leads me to hell. Or, I can take drastic action and go for surgery. Now, Jesus is not advocating self-mutilation here, but he is saying that sin is such a destructive force that there can be no negotiation with it. It is radioactive. We see that in the culture – sin attacks, people deny it, they explain it away but it attacks from underneath and does such horrific damage. You see, the Bible makes it clear: 'This is the verdict: light has come into the world, but people loved darkness instead of light because their deeds were evil' (John 3:19). This is the human heart.

So is hell for real? Yes, Jesus says so. What's it like? It's a sphere of punishment, separation, darkness and fire. Who is it for? It is for those who will not change, who will not submit to the God who gave them hands, feet, eyes and life. It is those who live as they please and say, 'I am an owner in God's world, I'm not a tenant. I'll kill the owner.' It's for those who won't have God as their God. That's who it's for.

And lastly, as we close, how can I escape if at all possible? Well, the good news is that it is possible to escape but in order to escape you have to have some sense of why it is so important that you should. You have to see the seriousness of going to this place where, verse 48, 'the worm does not die and the fire is not quenched'.

So if we see the danger of sin, how can we escape when it is this radioactive and dangerous? Well, the reason Jesus came into the world was to bear the hell that we deserve. He came in order that we might be saved from that awful destiny and rescued for the new creation with amazing, eternal bodies; no more weeping; no more sin or pain. Look at Keswick at its most beautiful and that will be nothing compared to what we will see in the new creation (1 Corinthians 2 verse 9).

Now there is no other explanation, no other reason for that terrible cry of Jesus on the afternoon of his crucifixion, 'My God, my God, why have you forsaken me?' (Matthew 27:46). Do you see what was happening there? He was entering into death, as the judgment of God against my sin, against what my hands and my feet and my eyes and my heart have done in his world. As all that sin is placed on him, so Jesus cries out, 'Why have I been forsaken by you?' And if there is anything to persuade you that the judgment of God is an awful thing to undergo then go to Calvary and hear him say, 'My God, my God, why have you forsaken me?' As Jesus experiences the essence of hell, the utter darkness, the weeping, the gnashing of teeth – in the depths of that cry piercing the Good Friday afternoon darkness – he provides the rescue from his plight, he opens the door to heaven and makes a way of escape. So as he cries, 'My God, my God why have I been forsaken?', you, through Christ, can gasp, 'My God, my God, why have I been accepted?'

Do you see that Jesus has loved us so much that he has been prepared, not only to enter our world, but, brothers and sisters, to go to the very depths of our hell in order to bring us up to heaven. And that is no small thing. It was William Booth of the Salvation Army, a great preacher to men and women, who said:

> Jesus Christ, by his death, offered a sacrifice for the sins of men which was of sufficient value to make amends

> for the damage done to the honour of the Law by man's transgression. This made it possible for God to forgive the sins of all who truly repent and believe in his Son and determine to lead lives of faith and obedience.[1]

So I want to say to you there is only one way to hell. The only way you get to hell is to trample over the cross of Jesus. He blocks the way. He says, 'I do not want you to go there. I've come to die to pay for your sin. But if you want to go to hell then you must trample over my cross.' God does not want you to go there. He so loved the world that he sent his Son to die for you. He is holy so sin must be judged, but he sent his Son to be judged. Do you know a hundred years ago, preachers would frequently finish their sermon by asking this question, 'Where will you spend eternity?' By God's grace, may there be no doubt what the answer might be to that question.

Note

1. William Booth, *The Atonement of Jesus Christ* (Lulu.com, 2015), p. 7.

How Can I Keep Going?

by Jeremy McQuoid

Jeremy McQuoid is the Teaching Pastor at Deeside Christian Fellowship in Aberdeen. He speaks at various conferences across the UK and is a trustee of the Pathways conference in Scotland, which seeks to train up a new generation of gospel workers. He is co-author of *The Amazing Cross*, part of the Keswick Foundation Series, along with his wife Elizabeth, a Keswick trustee. They have three sons.

How Can I Keep Going?
Hebrews 12:1–13

I don't know how many of you have seen the movie *Dead Poets Society*. The film is about an English teacher, played by Robin Williams, who is working in a very conservative, traditional school. And he ruffles feathers because he has unusual ways of inspiring his pupils. The scene I remember most is when he takes his pupils out of their regular class and leads them to a corridor in the school where there is an old, grainy, black and white photograph of former pupils.

He asks the boys to look into the eyes of these star pupils from the past. Their clothes are different, their hairstyles are different, but deep down they are just the same kind of boys, with just the same kind of dreams and ambitions. And while they are staring at this photo, Robin Williams whispers in Latin the phrase *carpe diem*, 'seize the day'. This is now your day. This is your time to make the most of your life. Be inspired by these former students. Go and live a glorious life.

And that's very much how Hebrews 12 begins. In Hebrews 11 the writer presents us with a kind of grainy photograph of men and women from the Old Testament who showed extraordinary faith, who trusted in the unseen promises of God, and clung to Christ in the face of massive obstacles. And now it's our turn. As we think about Noah and Moses, Abraham and David, perhaps even as we think of parents and grandparents, loved ones long gone, who walked with Jesus, and set a shining example for us, the Holy Spirit whispers to you and me, *carpe diem*, 'seize the day'. It's your turn. Go and live an extraordinary life of faith.

But the writer warns us that we will not find this life of faith any easier to live than those who went before us. These men and women wandered around in sheepskins and goatskins, persecuted and mistreated. Men and women of whom the world was not worthy (Hebrews 11:28). The life of faith is not a glamorous life. It's a life with great obstacles, and deep questions. And if we're going to live this life of faith, and reach the prize, then we need to run our race with perseverance.

Run our race with perseverance (verses 1–3)

That's what the writer is saying at the beginning of this passage. Verse 1:

> Therefore, since we are surrounded by such a great cloud of witnesses [these Old Testament heroes who are cheering us on], let us throw off everything that hinders and the sin that so easily entangles. And let us run with perseverance the race marked out for us.

The Christian life is a race. But it's not a glamorous sprint, it's a marathon that calls for endurance. In fact it's more like a steeplechase with obstacles that can knock us off track. I'm sure you've seen a steeplechase where you need all the grit of a long distance runner, but you need to be able to cope with jumping barriers, and dropping into water, and losing your rhythm along the way. That's what the life of faith is like.

And the writer says, if we are going to run this race with perseverance, we need to 'throw off everything that hinders and the sin that so easily entangles.' The word for 'everything that hinders' is the Greek word for a weight. Something which weighs you down and holds you back in the race. What are those weights for you? What are the things that hold you back from living a life of faith? It could be anything. Is it your love of money? Jesus said that money is perhaps the single biggest danger to spiritual growth. 'The love of money is a root of all kinds of evil' (1 Timothy 6:10). 'It is easier for a camel to go through the eye of a needle than for someone who is rich to enter the kingdom of God' (Luke 18:25). It's very difficult to follow Christ single-mindedly, if you are constantly thinking about how much money you have or don't have. Love of money is a weight that you need to throw off if you are going to run with perseverance.

Perhaps that weight is a specific sin that you keep indulging in. Perhaps pornography or, if not pornography itself, at least a careless thought-life that you keep indulging in – watching movies you shouldn't, browsing websites you shouldn't. If the statistics are right, this is one of the major problems facing the church. You can have very godly ambitions, and even be in a significant leadership position, but the one thing missing is dealing with your unhealthy thought-world.

Is the weight simply a lack of discipline? It's not that there is some great sin to confront, but your Christian living is just careless. Your Bible times are inconsistent, your prayer life is sporadic, and you never really wrestle with God in prayer. You don't mean to drift, but time just gets away from you. Too much time on Facebook, following a sport's team, making an idol out of your grandchildren, or obsessing about having an idyllic garden. Better to have a messy garden and a soul on fire, than an idyllic garden and a messy soul! None of these things are evil in themselves, but your lack of discipline is a weight that's holding you back from running your race with perseverance. The writer wants us to watch out for sins that so easily 'entangle' – the subtle sins of wealth, a porn-affected thought-life, and straight-forward ill-discipline that snares you like a spider silently weaving its web around your heart.

It's time to cast off those weights and run with perseverance the race marked out for you. You could translate verse 1, 'run your particular race'. If we are going to run with perseverance, not only do we need to cast off the things that hinder, but we need to run the race that God has prepared specifically for us. This is such a huge stumbling block for Christians. We take our eyes off our own race, because we're so busy analysing others around us.

Why can't I have the money he has? Why do I have to suffer and she doesn't? Why are my kids so hard to deal with and theirs seem idyllic? We have this tendency to look over the garden fence at others who seem to have a much easier race. Like Peter, when Jesus tells him he's going to die as a martyr, his first instinct is to look over at John and say, 'Lord, what about him?' (John 21:21). Of course John was the only disciple who wasn't martyred and lived to old age. But Jesus says to Peter, verse 22, 'What is that to you?' Essentially Jesus tells Peter to stop worrying about everyone else, run the race I have marked out for you. Stop looking over the fence.

If we want to run with perseverance, we need to set aside the weights that entangle us, we need to run our particular race, and, above all, we need to look to Jesus as we run. Jesus is our inspiration for the race. We are to run, verse 2:

> Fixing our eyes on Jesus, the pioneer and perfecter of faith. For the joy that was set before him he endured the cross, scorning its shame, and sat down at the right hand of the throne of God.

The writer wants to make sure we don't spend too long looking at Old Testament heroes of the faith who have come and gone. David Gooding writes, 'When all the vast army of witnesses has gone past, there comes one at last who takes our attention away from all else and fastens it on himself.'[1] Jesus our 'pioneer' has blazed a trail for us to follow. The great heroes of faith are in our rear view mirror, but Jesus is right in front of us beckoning us forward to follow where he has already gone.

Think of the sheer manly determination of Jesus to finish the race and fulfil his Father's plan. He sets his face to go to Jerusalem, where he knows he is going to be tortured and killed. Three times he predicts his death to his disciples but he steels himself to do it. And even in Gethsemane when he cries out to have the agony of the cross removed he still says, 'Yet not as I will, but as you will' (Matthew 26:39).

He allows men to strip him naked and whip him till the flesh is hanging off him. He carries his cross until he stumbles. He opens his hands to the nails, and his soul to the wrath of God. And he never takes a backward step: 'Hallelujah! what a Saviour!'[2] He is our inspiration to run the race. Jesus, our Pioneer. He sweated, bled, groaned, strived, wept and died for you. And best of all, he has now gone to the glory that you will go to as well. He is now seated at the right hand of God. His race is run. The cross before the crown, and that's what it will be for every child of God who perseveres by faith during the trials, questions, the mystery and often rejection of this life. We carry a cross today so that we will wear a crown in glory!

Run with perseverance the race marked out for you. That means setting aside all the things that are hindering your race. It means running your own particular race rather than worrying about what God is doing with others, and it means fixing your sights on Jesus, who has carried his cross ahead of us, and is now wearing a crown. *Carpe diem*. Seize the day. That's the call the writer wants to give to each of us tonight.

But now in the rest of this passage, the writer wants to say two things about our attitude as we run this race. Firstly, we need to submit to God's discipline as we run our race, and secondly we need to pursue God's best as we run our race. One is a passive stance – submitting to God's correction – and the other is an active stance – pursuing God's best.

Submit to God's discipline (verses 4–11)

Christians who have the expectation that life with God will be full of triumph will eventually hit the buffers. They don't understand God's purposes. These Jewish Christians in Hebrews were thinking of giving up the faith because they were facing persecution that wasn't part of their plan. So the writer wants to change their naïve expectations and help them to see God's hand, even in their sufferings.

Verses 5–6:

> Have you completely forgotten this word of encouragement that addresses you as a father addresses his son? It says,
>
> 'My son, do not make light of the Lord's discipline,
> and do not lose heart when he rebukes you,
> because the Lord disciplines the one he loves,
> and he chastens everyone he accepts as his son.'

God is a father who disciplines us in the same way a loving earthly father disciplines his children. In our home there isn't a week goes by where we don't say some stern words of rebuke to our boys, take away some of their treats, or give them a hard time about the lack of effort they've put into their homework. 'If you don't shape up, you'll have less time on the PlayStation. You'll have to miss football practice', or when things get really bad, 'You have to go shopping with us!' Is that because we don't love our kids, or because we do love them? Loving parents need to discipline their children because every child has rough edges to their character that need to be chipped off. There needs to be discipline.

God is our father but he's not a sugar daddy. He is a wise father who wants to produce maturity in us. So God will rebuke us if we're going in the wrong direction. He will use life circumstances to discipline us – perhaps a health issue, or a failed job interview, or a family crisis of some sort. John Calvin once said, 'The scourges of God are more useful to us because when God indulges us, we abuse his clemency and flatter ourselves and grow hardened in our sin.'[3] God allows everything that ever happens to us, even the painful events, and he has a purpose for it all. Allowing pain doesn't mean that God has stopped loving us, rather that he loves us so much he won't allow us to settle happily in ungodliness.

Verse 7:

> Endure hardship as discipline; God is treating you as his children.

That is the strange encouragement of this passage. The fact we go through hard times proves to us that God is our Father. He wants to refine us rather than indulge us. You cannot reach maturity without painful moments. This is how God reveals his Fatherhood to us, and chisels out Christlikeness in us. God loves us too much to leave us the way we are. C. S. Lewis famously said, 'God whispers to us in our pleasures, speaks in our consciences, but shouts in our pains: it is his megaphone to rouse a deaf world.'[4] And so many of the great Christians of the past have been refined by God-ordained pain.

William Carey was a great missionary to India who devoted much of his life to translating the Bible into various Indian languages. But on 11 March 1812, disaster struck. Carey was teaching in Calcutta. While he was gone, a fire started in the printing room of the large warehouse where all his translation work was done. Despite many hours of exhausting effort to fight the fire, the building burned to the ground. Just five pieces of equipment were saved. Carey's entire library, his completed Sanskrit dictionary, part of his Bengal dictionary, two grammar books, and ten translations of the Bible were lost. Gone also were the type sets for printing fourteen different languages. Vast quantities of English paper, priceless dictionaries, deeds, and account books were all gone.

When Carey surveyed the scene, he wept and said:

> In one night the labours of years are consumed. How unsearchable are the divine ways! I had lately brought some things to the utmost perfection I could, and contemplated the Mission with perhaps, too much self-congratulation. The Lord has laid me low, that I may look more simply to him.[5]

Carey was aware that he was too proud of the translation work he had done, and God had to tear it all down, to give him a fresh perspective. Will you submit to God's discipline? He is a loving father, refining you through it. Don't harbour bitterness, but understand that God loves you through the pain. He lays you low, and uses the pain to chisel away at your character until you look more and more like Jesus.

So the writer of Hebrews is calling us to run with perseverance the race marked out for us. And, as we run our race, we need to develop two attitudes: one is a passive attitude – we need to submit to God's discipline; the other is an active attitude – we need to pursue God's best.

Pursue God's best (verses 12–17)

There are a whole series of warnings throughout the book of Hebrews. The first one is the most famous: 'How shall we escape if we ignore so great a salvation?' (Hebrews 2:3). And the final warning in the book comes in the shape of a famous Old Testament story; Esau selling his birth right for a bowl of stew. If you remember the story, Jacob got the inheritance, simply because he wanted it more. He didn't go about it the right way – he connived with his mother to trick Isaac into giving him the blessing. But the lengths Jacob was prepared to go to get the blessing showed that he wanted it more than Esau.

Look at verses 15–16:

> See to it that no one falls short of the grace of God . . .
> or is godless like Esau, who for a single meal sold his
> inheritance rights as the oldest son.

Don't take God's grace lightly, is the idea. Don't treat it with contempt.

We're going to be moving into communion shortly, and the table spread before us reminds us of the tremendous cost of Calvary, and the glorious thing we are sharing in as we celebrate our salvation. Yes, we receive that grace freely. But surely the sign that we have truly been saved by grace is that God's grace becomes wonderful to us. God's grace compels us to give him not our scraps, but our very best. The gospel is like a treasure hidden in a field, and the man sells everything he has to gain the treasure.

If we know that we are recipients of God's grace through the broken body and poured-out blood of Christ; if we know that our earthly race, with all its tears and triumphs, will end in glory, in the company of thousands upon thousands of angels in joyful assembly, in the New Jerusalem, the City of God; if we know all this, then surely it should set our hearts on fire to pursue God's best?

Esau gave up his glorious birth right, and all the privileges it gave him, for a bowl of stew. He preferred to satisfy short-term physical desires, at the expense of long-term spiritual ones. Don't make the same mistake. Set out your stall for the kingdom that is to come. And if you have to sacrifice the short-term pleasures that money, sex, career and esteem can give you, then sacrifice them. Because the prize at the end of the race is so glorious. It will make your greatest moments in this world, your most magical times, seem like dust in the desert by comparison.

Paul said, 'I consider my life worth nothing to me; my only aim is to finish the race and complete the task the Lord Jesus has given me' (Acts 20:24). You have far more to run towards than you are leaving behind. Don't let short-term pleasures dim the glow of the heavenly city to come. Go back home after this Convention ready to serve like you have never done before; ready to witness with renewed courage; ready to worship with greater joy; ready to pray with greater zeal; ready to suffer if that is what it takes; ready to set aside everything that smacks of temporary, flesh-driven, pleasure-seeking, so that you can pursue Spirit-driven, gospel living, as you fix your eyes on the glory to come.

C. S. Lewis likened our lives on this earth, however long and often painful they may be, to the preface of a book. When we get to glory we'll begin the real story, where each chapter is better than the one before.[6] Run your race with perseverance, submit to God's discipline along the way, and pursue God's best. Don't stagger through the finish line of life with deep regret because you ran a half-hearted race. Run through the tape, with arms aloft, and wait for Christ to place a glittering crown on your head. *Carpe diem*. Seize the day.

Notes

1. David Gooding, *An Unshakeable Kingdom: the Letter to the Hebrews for Today Volume 5* (Myrtlefield House, 2013), p. 224.
2. Philip Bliss, 'Man of sorrows', 1875.
3. Iain Duguid, *Ezekiel* NIV *commentary* (Zondervan, 1999), p. 71.
4. C. S. Lewis, *The Problem of Pain* (William Collins, 2015), p. 92.
5. S. Pearce Carey and Peter Masters, *William Carey* (Wakeman Trust, 2008), p. 290.
6. C. S. Lewis, *The Last Battle* (HarperCollins, 2001), p. 222.

Keswick Resources
Enjoy the 2016 Convention!

All the teaching from Keswick 2016 is available, and here are the various options available to you:

1. Free mp3 downloads of Bible readings, evening celebrations and lectures

Please go to the Keswick Ministries website and listen to or download the mp3s. All you need to do is register, and then all downloads are free of charge. Here's the link: https://keswickministries.org/resources/keswick-talk-downloads.

2. Essential Christian

All teaching – Bible readings, evening celebrations, seminars and lectures – is available in various formats, including CD, DVD, mp3 and also USB stick. These can be purchased from Essential Christian. Please go to www.essentialchristian.com/keswick.

Other Keswick teaching is also available from this site, and you can browse the Bible teaching catalogue as far back as 1957! You can also browse albums by worship leaders and artists who have performed at Keswick, including Stuart Townend, Keith and Kristen Getty, plus Keswick Live albums and collections of popular DVDs. To order, visit www.essentialchrisitian.com/keswick or call 0845 607 1672.

3. Free online viewing of Bible readings and lectures
Keswick Convention Bible readings and lectures are also available on Clayton TV at www.clayton.tv. Select what you would like to see, and watch the talks online.

Please encourage others to benefit from these Keswick resources.

Thank you!

KESWICK MINISTRIES

Our purpose

Keswick Ministries is committed to the spiritual renewal of God's people for his mission in the world.

God's purpose is to bring his blessing to all the nations of the world. That promise of blessing, which touches every aspect of human life, is ultimately fulfilled through the life, death, resurrection, ascension and future return of Christ. All of the people of God are called to participate in his missionary purposes, wherever he may place them. The central vision of *Keswick Ministries* is to see the people of God equipped, encouraged and refreshed to fulfil that calling, directed and guided by God's Word in the power of his Spirit, for the glory of his Son.

Our priorities

Keswick Ministries seeks to serve the local church through:

- ***Hearing God's Word***: the Scriptures are the foundation for the church's life, growth and mission, and *Keswick Ministries* is committed to preach and teach God's Word in a way that is faithful to Scripture and relevant to Christians of all ages and backgrounds.

- ***Becoming like God's Son***: from its earliest days the Keswick movement has encouraged Christians to live godly lives in the power of the Spirit, to grow in Christlikeness and to live under his lordship in every area of life. This is God's will for his people in every culture and generation.
- ***Serving God's mission***: the authentic response to God's Word is obedience to his mission, and the inevitable result of Christlikeness is sacrificial service. *Keswick Ministries* seeks to encourage committed discipleship in family life, work and society, and energetic engagement in the cause of world mission.

Our ministry

Keswick: the event. Every summer the town of Keswick hosts a three-week Convention, which attracts some 15,000 Christians from the UK and around the world. The event provides Bible teaching for all ages, vibrant worship, a sense of unity across generations and denominations, and an inspirational call to serve Christ in the world. It caters for children of all ages and has a strong youth and young adult programme. And it all takes place in the beautiful Lake District – a perfect setting for rest, recreation and refreshment.

Keswick: the movement. For 140 years the work of Keswick has impacted churches worldwide, and today the movement is underway throughout the UK, as well as in many parts of Europe, Asia, North America, Australia,

Africa and the Caribbean. *Keswick Ministries* is committed to strengthen the network in the UK and beyond, through prayer, news, pioneering and cooperative activity.

Keswick resources. *Keswick Ministries* is producing a growing range of books and booklets based on the core foundations of Christian life and mission. It makes Bible teaching available through free access to mp3 downloads, and the sale of DVDs and CDs. It broadcasts online through Clayton TV and annual BBC Radio 4 services. In addition to the summer Convention, Keswick Ministries is hoping to develop other teaching and training events in the coming years.

Our unity

The Keswick movement worldwide has adopted a key Pauline statement to describe its gospel inclusivity: 'for you are all one in Christ Jesus' (Galatians 3:28). *Keswick Ministries* works with evangelicals from a wide variety of church backgrounds, on the understanding that they share a commitment to the essential truths of the Christian faith as set out in our statement of belief.

Our contact details

T: 01768 780075
E: info@keswickministries.org
W: www.keswickministries.org
Mail: Keswick Ministries, Convention Centre, Skiddaw Street, Keswick CA12 4BY, England